Liberating the Land

Two week
~n

Please return on or before the la
date stamped below

Liberating the Land

The Case for Private Land-use Planning

MARK PENNINGTON

The Institute of Economic Affairs

First published in Great Britain in 2002 by
The Institute of Economic Affairs
2 Lord North Street
Westminster
London sw1P 3LB
in association with Profile Books Ltd

A CIP catalogue record for this book is available from the British Library.

ISBN 0 255 36508 X

Many IEA publications are translated into languages other than English or are
reprinted. Permission to translate or to reprint should be sought from the
General Director at the address above.

Typeset in Stone by MacGuru
info@macguru.org.uk

Printed and bound in Great Britain by Hobbs the Printers

CONTENTS

THE AUTHOR

Dr Mark Pennington is Lecturer in Public Policy in the Department of Politics at Queen Mary College, University of London. Prior to his current post he was a post-doctoral researcher in the Department of Geography and Environment at the London School of Economics and Political Science, following the completion of his doctorate in 1997. Dr Pennington has published widely on the political economy of environmental policy, including articles in journals such as *New Political Economy*, *Environmental Politics*, *Journal of Environmental Policy and Planning*, *Environment and Planning*, and *Policy and Politics*. For the IEA, he was the author of *Conservation and the Countryside: by quango or market?* (1996). His recent book *Planning and the Political Market: Public Choice and the Politics of Government Failure* (Athlone Press, London, 2000) is the first book-length analysis of the British town and country planning system from a public-choice perspective.

FOREWORD

I am pleased to write a few words about Mark Pennington's stimulating treatise. As a proud standard-bearer of that oxymoron field of 'libertarian planning', I was especially interested in his application of the principles of Hayek, public choice and Coase to the issue of local land-use planning. I have dabbled with those ideas myself, but not with such thoroughness. Like Dr Pennington, I have also been somewhat perplexed by the move towards liberalisation at the global and national levels, combined with a simultaneous emphasis on increased regulation with respect to local land use.

To inject a personal note, I left the United Kingdom more than a generation ago for the 'land of the free', only to find, year by year, the increasing encroachment of command-and-control, social engineering and environmental fascism on the exercise of local private property rights. The major difference between the United Kingdom and the United States, of course, is that while in the United Kingdom local authorities grant planning permission under strict Department of the Environment guidelines, in the United States land-use planning is, theoretically at least, in the hands of individual local jurisdictions, although in many instances they have to conform to state laws (but these also vary, often substantially, from state to state). Nevertheless, bad ideas (like growth controls and 'smart' – think 'dumb' – growth ordinances) spread like forest fires, while good ideas (like transferable development rights) exist on paper in many cities and counties but languish from neglect. So, Dr Pennington's views are as relevant to the United States' situation as they are to that in the United Kingdom.

Space prohibits more than a sentence or two devoted to arguments that merit much more attention. The Hayekian case for the spontaneous order generated by market decentralisation is even stronger now because, to the extent that organised information is relevant to decision-making, it has been democratised via the Internet. Now, within a few minutes, any individual or market agent has access to information that would formerly have taken a planning authority months to acquire. There can be little doubt that New Towns programmes in the United Kingdom and elsewhere contribute to sprawl and excess commuting, but few have pointed this out as clearly as Dr Pennington. Similarly with the Green Belts: ignoring the wide variation in the environmental quality of land within the Green Belts is a particularly irritating example of government failure. Placing all this discussion in the context of planning paradigms (such as rational, incrementalist and collaborative – or participatory – planning) is also helpful, especially for students.

Another very interesting application of broader conceptual frameworks to land-use planning by Dr Pennington is his treatment of public-choice theory. The rational ignorance stance adopted by citizen-voters allows politicians to pander to special-interest groups. The result is development restrictions that raise the price of residential land and housing. A similar example is the opposition to Walmarts and hypermarkets; however, this is as prevalent in the United States as in the United Kingdom. The lesson is that local government tyranny can be as oppressive as centralised tyranny. Also, the beauty of the Tiebout model becomes a little tarnished in practice. I suspect that Dr Pennington looks across the Atlantic through rose-tinted glasses. I hate to prick the bubble of his youthful idealism, but from this old cynic's perspective decentralisation may improve the situation but it is far from an ideal solution. The 'herd instinct' is compelling. The emphasis on creating and enforcing private property rights suggested by Dr Pennington is a far more attractive approach. However, the prospects for implementation remain problematic. I am probably more sympathetic to the expansion of market-based land-use planning instruments (such as tradable permits and development rights auctions) than Dr Pennington because it involves building on strategies that are already in place (at least in the United States) rather than striking out in uncharted territory.

The final theme in Dr Pennington's trenchant analysis is his extension of Coasian ideas. He gives most attention to what he calls the common property regime under which homeowners (and commercial establishments) join together in a private covenant to adopt certain rules to maintain their joint property values. The homeowner association rules (called CC&Rs, i.e. Covenants, Conditions and Restrictions) govern what homeowners can and cannot do. The idea is fine in theory, but less so in practice. If the tyranny of central government is bad, and local government tyranny is worse, there is no more dangerous tyranny than that of your neighbours in the form of a Homeownership Association Board. I know; I live under such an oligarchy. HOA rules dictate what flowers you can grow in your front garden, the colour of your curtains, the length of time your garage door can be kept open. A particularly egregious example occurred after the World Trade Center horror, when many Americans wanted to empathise by displaying the American flag. They were forced to take it down because, according to most CC&Rs, it is a 'lawn ornament'.

As some of the above comments suggest, I am not fully convinced of the practicality of some of Dr Pennington's proposals. Nevertheless, his analysis stimulated me to think more about them. I hope it will stimulate you as much. This is one of the most valuable dissections of land-use regulatory planning regimes to be published in recent years.

HARRY W. RICHARDSON

Professor of Planning and Economics in the School of Policy, Planning and

Development, University of Southern California

February 2002

As with all IEA publications, the views expressed in Dr Pennington's paper are those of the author, not those of the Institute (which has no corporate view), its managing trustees, Academic Advisory Council or senior staff.

ACKNOWLEDGEMENTS

I take this opportunity to thank two anonymous referees for some extremely useful comments, which have been reflected in the finished text. Professor Colin Robinson is owed special thanks for invaluable editorial support and patience. Thanks are also due to John and Christine Blundell for their ever-present support and encouragement, and my colleagues at Queen Mary, for providing such a friendly and stimulating place at which to work. Finally, I would like to thank my friends, especially Catarina Cardoso, Dan Graham and Steven Whitehill, for their continuing tolerance.

I would also like to thank Profile Books for finding the splendid cover illustration of Letchworth – the first 'garden city' built in the UK, and financed through co-operative private enterprise.

Any errors within the text are mine and mine alone.

MARK PENNINGTON

February 2002

SUMMARY

- Despite the apparent acceptance of market forces and the 'rhetoric of deregulation', governments regulate many activities closely, including the management of land-use change.
- The ownership and use of land in the United Kingdom are now '... subject to a greater array of statutory controls than at any time since the introduction of the 1947 Town and Country Planning Act', partly because of pressure from 'environmentalists'.
- 'Market failure' arguments are used to support the case for land-use planning. Markets are said to neglect third-party effects, to be short-termist, and to fail to provide adequate information. Government agencies can, it is claimed, overcome these problems and also deal with distributional issues.
- A Hayekian perspective shows the error of such arguments. It is impossible for planners to gather and interpret the information that would be required to operate an efficient land-use planning system. The constant feedback provided by changing relative prices in a market is needed to utilise dispersed knowledge and to facilitate adjustment.
- The planning case looks weaker still when seen from a public-

choice viewpoint. Planners are not motivated solely by the desire to serve the 'public interest', and they are subject to pressure from special-interest groups which have in Britain, *inter alia*, helped create an artificial scarcity of land and rising prices. Political short-termism and bureaucratic expansionism are also entrenched in the system.

- The present British land-use planning system suffers from serious institutional deficiencies – over-centralisation, absence of experimentation, lack of information and inappropriate incentive structures.

- Decentralisation of planning powers to local authorities might help, especially if there were a return to locally raised taxation, but more fundamental reform introducing a Hayekian discovery process is required.

- Introducing direct financial compensation to those adversely affected by developments and auctioning development rights might also help improve the system, but such measures do not address the fundamental flaw in the present regime – that development rights are nationalised.

- Supposed 'market failures' in land use are primarily the result of the high cost of enforcing property rights, but these costs can be reduced by entrepreneurial action in a market. For example, private covenants and deed restrictions can be used to preserve open spaces, to avoid nuisances of various kinds and to maintain scenic views. Proprietary communities also provide a means of internalising local external effects and would lower the costs of dealing with externalities that go beyond the local area.

- A private system of land-use control, using proprietary governance, though a radical departure, would be a considerable advance on the present regime. One way to move to such a system would be to establish local recreation and amenity companies which would hold development rights collectively.

Liberating the Land

1 INTRODUCTION

In recent years the political economy of the United Kingdom has been subject to many institutional changes, foremost of which has been a redrawing of the boundaries between the private market and the state. Where once the assumption was that the trend towards greater state ownership and to progressively higher levels of government spending was irreversible, there is now acceptance (though often grudging) of the importance of allowing market forces to operate at least *relatively* freely.

Notwithstanding these trends, it is far from clear that the institutional changes towards a more liberal market order which have occurred in the recent past are irreversible. 'Anti-capitalist' protests aside, whilst it is now rare to hear calls for the 'nationalisation of industry' and for 'conscious direction' of the economy, the talk increasingly is of the need for the state to *regulate* markets more closely and for governments to spend money where it is thought that markets cannot operate effectively. As Milton Friedman has put it, 'On both sides of the Atlantic, it is only a little overstated to say that we preach individualism and market capitalism and continue to practice socialism.'[1]

One area of contemporary public policy where it is indeed

---

1   M. Friedman, Introduction to the 50th Anniversary Edition of Friedrich Hayek (1944), *The Road to Serfdom*, Chicago University Press, Chicago, 1995, p. xxvii.

perhaps only a little overstated to suggest that we continue to 'practise socialism' is in the management of land-use change.[2] In spite of the rhetoric of deregulation that has characterised much of the last twenty years, at present the ownership and use of land in the United Kingdom *is subject to a greater array of statutory controls than at any time since the introduction of the 1947 Town and Country Planning Act.* Contemporary pressure for more regulation has been heightened with the rise of the environmental agenda. For many in the green movement and in the public media more generally, the thought of allowing land uses to be allocated according to the principles of supply and demand and of voluntary contract is anathema. Whether it is to save the countryside from the threat of urban sprawl, or in response to the need to regenerate the inner cities, politicians of all parties are quick to call for *more* regulation.

As is the tradition of IEA publications, this paper seeks to 'think the unthinkable' and thus to put the case for a private system of land-use control. Having sketched out the key arguments that are advanced in favour of statutory land-use regulation, the paper throws doubt on the claims that are currently made for a more 'integrated land-use policy'. In doing so, the analysis builds on three traditions of thought that have been a common theme in many of the Institute's publications. Section 3 uses the principles of the Hayekian/Austrian school to demonstrate some of the fundamental informational deficiencies of government land-use plan-

---

2   It has been suggested by a referee that such a characterisation would not be recognised by British Conservative governments in the post-1951 era, let alone by the Thatcher administrations of the 1980s, all of which persisted with a commitment to the British land-use planning system. In response, it is worth recalling that Hayek's 1944 text was addressed to the socialists of *all* parties and that we should not confuse the rhetorical commitment of politicians to the market economy with the reality of their actions on the ground.

ning. Section 4 uses public-choice theory to explore deficiencies in the incentive structures characteristic of the planning regime. Building on the Hayekian and public-choice analyses, Section 5 considers some suggestions for reforming the existing planning system from within. Section 6, meanwhile, draws on the Coasian or property rights tradition to outline the theoretical case for the total *replacement of government land-use planning* with a market-driven system of land-use control. Section 7 concludes the analysis with some practical proposals for institutional reform, focusing on the possibility of a radical privatisation of development rights at both the individual and the neighbourhood/community level.

2 THE ALLURE OF GOVERNMENT LAND-USE PLANNING

The British land-use planning system constitutes one of the most comprehensive systems of government land-use regulation anywhere in the industrialised world. Following the 1947 Town and Country Planning Act virtually all non-agricultural uses of land have been subject to the requirement to obtain planning permission as a direct consequence of the nationalisation of development rights. Anyone wishing to develop his or her property must apply for planning permission to a local planning authority, which must decide the application on the basis of the land-use strategy set out in either a local district plan, county structure plan or unitary development plan. These plans, meanwhile, are themselves developed on the basis of guidelines laid down by the Department of the Environment, Food and Rural Affairs (previously the Department of the Environment, Transport and the Regions), where the Secretary of State holds the power to 'call in' plans that are judged not to be in accordance with national guidance contained within Planning Policy Guidance Notes (PPGs).

Land-use planning – too important to be left to the market

The common assumption underlying the continued political support for such comprehensive land-use regulation is that the allocation of land uses and of environmental resources more generally is 'too important to be left to the market'. Seen from this perspective, even if it is accepted that the production of most of the commodities that make up the general standard of living can safely be left to the profit-seeking sector, land is a 'special case' where market forces cannot be trusted to operate effectively. The pattern of land use that constitutes both rural and urban environments is, according to advocates of statutory land-use planning, a crucial element in the public 'quality of life' which simply cannot be left to the vagaries of competition. Whether it is the need to protect the aesthetic qualities of the countryside from the threat of 'urban sprawl', or the desire to preserve the fabric of our towns and cities, these are matters that are best left to the benevolent patrimony of the state and not to the whims and fancies of 'selfish' individuals.[1]

The mistrust of market forces in the environmental sphere and the allure of land-use planning in particular owe much to the 'market failure' orthodoxy of modern welfare economics.[2] Advocates of greater regulation are united in the view that land-use issues exhibit various 'externality' and 'public good' characteristics that prevent the effective operation of private markets. According to this perspective, private individuals/property owners are *not* held sufficiently to account for the consequences of their actions in land

---

1   See, for example, Department of the Environment, *Sustainable Development: The UK Strategy*, HMSO, London, 1994.

2   Market failure arguments for environmental regulation can be found in a variety of textbooks on environmental economics. For more specific applications to land-use planning, see, for example, A. Harrison, *Economics and Land Use Planning*, Policy Journals, Newbury, 1977; C. Whitehead, 'The Rationale for Government Intervention', in H. B. Dunkerley (ed.), *Urban Land Policy: Issues and Opportunities*, Oxford University Press, Oxford, 1983; R. Klosterman, 'Arguments for and against Planning', *Town Planning Review*, vol. 56, no. 1, 1985.

markets. Externality and collective goods problems mean that 'countryside goods' and other environmental amenities will be 'under-produced' if competitive market forces are allowed a free rein. Private developers will, for example, fail to take into account the negative externalities associated with urban sprawl and loss of open spaces, as these are not reflected in the market price of new houses and other urban developments.

In addition to such basic instances of institutional failure associated with 'third-party effects', the operation of the market in land is considered to be afflicted with a range of related deficiencies that are thought to be in need of corrective government action. One of the most frequently cited arguments found in support of statutory land-use planning is the notion that market participants are chronically 'short-termist' in their outlook. The dominance of the profit motive, if left to operate freely, it is argued, will lead to the over-exploitation of environmental resources as property owners act according to their immediate financial interests, at the expense of future generations. Within this context, concerns that valuable agricultural land and open spaces will be irrevocably lost to urban development provide one of the most widely cited arguments for government land-use planning.

Yet another argument for intervention suggests that planning can improve the information that is available to market participants and hence smooth the operation of the market process itself. According to this view, in order for private actors to make successful investments a degree of 'certainty' is required concerning the land-use changes to be brought about by other actors operating in related markets. The requirement here is for knowledge about the likely intentions of other developers – their plans for future housing output, for example, the location of this output, and the likely implications of such decisions with regard to the provision of roads and other public infrastructure which may affect market conditions overall. Since land-use decisions may have a variety of 'knock-on' effects or 'network externalities' for a host of other decision-makers, the 'anarchic' decisions of dispersed private property owners will not be sufficiently co-ordinated without some form of central intervention. Land-use planning, therefore, is considered to have an important role to play in providing information to market participants about land-use trends, population patterns and public infrastructure decisions such as the provision of trunk roads, schools and hospitals, and in regulating the actions of private actors in order that they may be properly integrated with one another. In this way cycles of speculative 'boom and bust' in the property market can be avoided and inappropriate location choices (for example, building houses in areas with inadequate infrastructure provision) can be successfully minimised.

A final set of arguments for land-use planning is centred primarily on distributional concerns. Seen from this perspective government regulation is needed in order to ensure that those on low incomes are afforded a greater degree of access to environmental quality. Public planning is seen as an important means of 'empowering' low-income people by taking active measures to improve the quality of life in poorer areas and to redirect economic activity away from those locations in danger of 'overheating' towards those suffering from unemployment and other aspects of social deprivation.

Three models of government land-use planning

Notwithstanding the widespread acceptance of the need for some sort of public intervention to tackle instances of 'market failure', there is considerable disagreement among the supporters of government land-use planning about the institutional arrangements that are thought necessary to regulate land markets effectively. Broadly speaking, three traditions may be identified within contemporary planning theory, each with a distinctive view of the purpose of land-use planning and of the manner in which this planning should be carried out.

Much contemporary land-use planning theory continues to draw on the rationalist or procedural approach to public decision-making as advanced by authors such as Faludi.[3] Working within the rationalist tradition, Faludi makes a distinction between theories *for* planning and theories *of* planning.[4]

Theories *for* planning involve the development of techniques such as computer modelling, simulation and forecasting which are held to provide planners with a better understanding of the processes that they are seeking to manage – population trends, projected trends in industrial and residential location, projected environmental resource stocks, and so forth. Theories *of* planning, on the other hand, are concerned with the actual process of planning itself, and in particular the choice of 'optimal' ways of taking decisions in order to formulate solutions to pre-defined social goals. Within this context, the favoured decision tool was, and still is for many planning theorists, the comprehensive planning model. In this particular model, planners are assumed to be able to collect all the relevant 'data' and rationally devise a policy that will achieve the desired goal. As such, these models represent a

---

3   A. Faludi, *A Reader in Planning Theory*, Pergamon, Oxford, 1973.
4   ibid.

variant of the tradition of social cost/benefit analysis within neo-classical economics. If the market economy and the price system are thought not to respond effectively to individual preferences through the interaction of supply and demand, then land-use planners, appropriately trained in the best 'scientific' methods of preference assessment, are required to step in to perform this co-ordinating role. The task of the land-use planner, therefore, is to deploy a range of 'neutral' evaluation techniques in order objectively to identify and measure individual preferences for the relevant environmental goods.[5]

Incrementalist models of planning represent the second major strand in contemporary planning theory. Inspired by authors such as Lindblom, this approach developed out of a critique of the rationalist/procedural model, which was thought unrealistic in its assumptions about the ability of planners to collect and centralise all the necessary data and to foresee the *unintended* consequences of policy implementation.[6] According to Lindblom and his followers, planning should be seen more as a process of *disjointed incrementalism*. Planners *do not* know all the necessary information for effective decision-making in advance but acquire information over time through a process of trial and error, 'learning by doing'. Rather than achieving the objectives of planning via the adoption of a comprehensive model, policies edge forward over time in a series of smaller incremental steps not dissimilar to Popper's notion of 'piecemeal interventionism'. In this model of planning, the

---

5   See, for example, D. Pearce, *et al.*, *Blueprint for a Green Economy*, Earthscan, London, 1989.

6   See, for example, D. Braybrooke and C. Lindblom, *A Strategy of Decision: Policy Evaluation as a Social Process*, Collier-Macmillan, London, 1963; C.Lindblom, *Politics and Markets*, Basic Books, New York, 1977.

knowledge that is necessary for effective decision-making is thought to be more dispersed than in the comprehensive rationalist approach. Rather than being centralised in a single 'super planning agency', the necessary knowledge is divided between a variety of agents which may include different government departments dealing with a range of policy areas, private-sector actors and various interest groups. Within this context the usual mechanisms of negotiative give and take in the political process are seen to provide the appropriate vehicle for bringing dispersed knowledge together and facilitating effective policy-making.

'Collaborative planning' represents the third major strand in contemporary planning theory, and constitutes the most radical attack on the technocratic, rationalist approach. According to authors such as Healey, the emphasis on objective, 'scientific' conceptions of knowledge in the rationalist approach acts to exclude other forms of knowledge, including tacit knowhow, practical 'commonsense reason' and appeals to moral or ethical claims that are *not* open to scientific measurement and quantification.[7]

From the perspective of collaborative planning, the claims to objectivity made by planning 'experts' are subject to serious limits. It is, for example, well accepted (even by their adherents) that the results of supposedly neutral techniques such as social cost/benefit analysis are in large part a reflection of *subjective value judgements* made by the planners concerned.[8] Whilst incrementalist planning is seen as representing an improvement on the comprehensive planning ideal, it too is viewed by collaborative planning theorists as privileging the role played by professional

---

7   P. Healey, *Collaborative Planning*, Macmillan, London, 1997.
8   R. Formaini, *The Myth of Scientific Public Policy*, Transaction Books, New York, 1991.

experts rather than drawing on the local/subjective knowledge of the public at large. The knowledge that needs to be taken into account by the planning process is, according to Healey and her followers, much more decentralised than in expert-centred traditions of planning theory. The ideal institutional environment for policy-making, therefore, requires a more participatory form of planning, where all the relevant 'stakeholders' are given a chance to have their say. Greater levels of public participation in decision-making are held to offer the prospect of 'citizen empowerment', reducing the likelihood of arbitrary bureaucratic rule and improving the accountability of the planning process by maximising the input of information that would not be available to technocratic experts acting alone.[9]

Land-use planning in Britain

Each of the theoretical approaches discussed above may be seen to have had an influence throughout the history of land-use planning in Britain, and in turn each of these approaches can be witnessed to a greater or lesser extent in the practice of planning today.

The British planning system has never approximated a 'centrally planned' or fully comprehensive system in the sense of *all* decisions being taken by a 'national bureau of land use' or equivalent. Rather, planning has operated within the context of a 'mixed-economy' model, with responsibilities divided between an array of government bodies, such as the Department of the Environment, Transport and the Regions, county and district planning authorities, and a range of quasi-autonomous bodies

---

9   Healey, op. cit.

such as English Nature and the Housing Corporation. With the exception of the period 1948–51, the process of land development has continued to be one where the majority of investment and production decisions are taken by private landowners and developers with the planning system operating to *regulate* such market activity rather than to direct and plan development *per se*.

These elements of decentralisation aside, however, the British planning system is indeed characterised by quite a high degree of centralisation (especially when compared to the position in the United States). The Department of the Environment, Food and Rural Affairs (DEFRA), in particular, continues to exert a high degree of national control through the issue of Planning Policy Guidance Notes and the 'call-in' powers of the Secretary of State. Many planning policies have been characterised by a distinct whiff of the comprehensive rationalist model. Technocratic arguments, for example, lay at the heart of the postwar commitment to a planned decentralisation of the urban population into self-contained 'New Towns', designed to reduce congestion in the older cities and at the same time ensure the protection of the countryside by concentrating development in targeted 'growth poles'. Combined with the rise of regional policy and the mass programme of slum clearance in the inner cities at the time, the New Towns policy represented perhaps the clearest manifestation of a belief in the power of 'expert' managers to direct the location of housing and industry in the name of 'public welfare'. The continued reliance on 'command-and-control' models of land-use policy today is evidenced by the persistence of policies such as Green Belts, which effectively *forbid* most forms of development in large swathes of land around the major towns and cities.

The incrementalist model of planning is perhaps most evident in the day-to-day procedure of development control, that is, the decisions made by planners at district and county level to grant or refuse individual planning applications and the bargaining that takes place between different agencies within the planning system. Whilst in theory the decision to grant or refuse an individual application is based on the policies laid out in structure or local plans and the constraints provided by national planning guidance, these plans are rarely set in stone. As will be noted subsequently, structure and local plans are far from the most flexible or up-to-date policy instruments, but it would be a mistake to suggest that they are totally lacking in flexibility. Local authority planners *do* exercise a considerable degree of discretion in the decisions they make, and as a consequence plans may change gradually over time as planners negotiate and engage with developers, other agencies within the public sector, and the day-to-day pressure of interest group politics.

The influence of the collaborative planning model, meanwhile, has become increasingly evident in recent years with a raft of government proposals designed to step up the level of public participation in decision-making. The 1971 Town and Country Planning Act introduced public participation into the planning process following the recommendations of the Skeffington Report (1969). This legislation extended the right of members of the public to make objections to the policies laid out in plans and for the first time to be consulted during the process of plan preparation itself. Such mechanisms were extended further in the 1991 Planning and Compensation Act, which saw a substantial increase in the length of the planning process due to the growing significance of public inquiries. Following its election in May 1997, the 'New Labour' administration has committed itself to the development of a range of participatory mechanisms such as 'citizens' juries', 'focus groups' and 'community workshops', designed to improve the responsiveness and accountability of the planning system as part of its intention to 'modernise' the structures of British government.

Whichever of these different planning models has been in the ascendancy, the common thread uniting supporters of government land-use planning has been the belief that greater regulation of markets provides the best way to improve environmental quality. Within this context, a continuing theme throughout the history of the planning system has been the constant striving for a more 'integrated', 'joined-up' or 'holistic' approach to land management. The most recent manifestation of this striving has been the call for the planning system to reorientate the urban system – moving it away from an emphasis on suburban developments, reliant on road transit and the private car, towards a more high-density, compacted form of development serviced by public transport. By reducing transport distances, it is suggested that 'integrated land-use planning' and more 'sustainable urban forms' can help to reduce the emittance of pollutants and 'greenhouse gases' such as carbon dioxide. It is these arguments which appear well to the fore in a host of government documents that speak freely of an important role for the land-use planning system in the attainment of 'sustainable development'.[10]

---

10 Department of the Environment, Transport and the Regions, *Modernising Planning*, HMSO, London, 1998. For more academic support see, for example, G. Haughton and C. Hunter, *Sustainable Cities*, Regional Studies Association/Jessica Kingsley, London, 1994; A. Blowers and B. Evans (eds), *Town Planning into the 21st Century*, Routledge, London, 1997.

3 HAYEKIAN OBJECTIONS TO GOVERNMENT LAND-USE PLANNING

To those used to thinking exclusively in 'market failure' terms, the arguments for land-use planning sketched in the previous section seem overwhelming. To those aware of the fundamental problems of government planning as a *genre*, however, the case for greater regulation is far from clear. Put simply, the key assumption underlying the case for government land-use planning is that the information needed to ensure that all potential uses of land are sufficiently 'integrated' with one another *can be made available to planners*. This is clearly the case with the 'expert'-centred tradition of the comprehensive rationalist model, but is only marginally less apparent in the 'incrementalist' and 'collaborative' planning approaches.

In the former case, it is assumed that while planners are not in possession of full information, they are able to acquire more information over time and to improve the effectiveness of their decisions through a process of trial-and-error learning. In the latter instance the assumption appears to be that if planners are able to hold sufficient committee meetings and encourage the general populace to participate in such gatherings then the dispersed knowledge that would be needed to achieve a more 'integrated land-use policy' could be gathered and distilled. In order to appreciate the *specific* difficulties inherent in each of these approaches to land-use planning it is first necessary to examine the *general* critique of government planning and the advocacy of market institutions put forward by Hayek.

Decentralised knowledge and the market as a discovery process

According to Hayek, much of the knowledge necessary for social and economic co-ordination is diffused throughout society, is to a large extent *subjective* and, far from being 'given', must be 'produced' through a process of trial-and-error learning.[1] Contrary to the assumptions of neoclassical welfare economics and other such rationalist models, objective knowledge of economic conditions is the exception rather than the rule. If a world of objectively given knowledge existed, then there would be no scope for individual choice, for people would have no option but to respond to the objective stimuli before them. Similarly, where preferences are assumed to be known and constant, the role of consumer is reduced to that of an automaton. If objective knowledge of relative resource scarcities and consumer preferences could be made available in 'scientific' form then it would indeed be possible to dispense with the market in favour of central planning and to have the allocation of resources supervised by government officials employing the techniques of social cost/benefit analysis.

From a Hayekian perspective, it is mistaken to cite examples of 'market failure' as a product of 'imperfect information', since a world of perfect foresight cannot exist under *any* institutional setting. The key question for political economy is to ascertain which institutions are best suited to operate in an uncertain world where the assumptions that underlie the rationalist model simply cannot exist in reality. The task of the political economist, therefore, is *not*

---

1   See, for example, the essays in F. A. Hayek, *Individualism and Economic Order*, Chicago University Press, Chicago, 1948; F. A. Hayek, 'Competition as a Discovery Procedure', in *New Studies in Politics, Economics and the History of Ideas*, Routledge, London, 1978.

to highlight the failure of social and economic institutions to attain a state of perfect co-ordination, but to provide explanations for the degree of co-ordination that we *do actually see*.[2]

For Hayekian political economy, it is precisely because values and knowledge are to a significant extent *subjective*, and information diffuse and uncertain, that government planning is unlikely to succeed. This is not to say that *no* objective information may be obtained in a centralised form (such as information about population patterns and previous land-use trends, for example), but that even in the presence of such data different individuals will interpret the implications to be obtained from the same data in different ways. Individual choice is a creative act, which takes place under conditions of imperfect information, chronic uncertainty and with the distinct possibility of error. Entrepreneurs operating in the market *do not* start from a position of knowing what goods to produce, in what quantities and at what price to sell, but are faced with a situation where they must acquire such knowledge *over time*. Similarly, consumers *do not* necessarily start from a position of 'knowing what they want', but are constantly re-evaluating their preferences as the process of entrepreneurial experimentation in the market unwinds. Given the 'social division of knowledge', the purpose of a competitive market system is to test out a variety of competing ideas, dispersed amongst a myriad of individuals and firms, in order to discover and rediscover which of these ideas dovetails most closely with those of their fellows.

From a Hayekian perspective, planners (democratically elected or otherwise) can never perceive and respond to as many

---

2   P. Boettke, 'Where Did Economics Go Wrong?', *Critical Review*, vol. 11, 1997, pp. 10–64.

instances of dis-coordination as can individuals who have the freedom to exchange property titles in the market. Where production possibilities and consumer preferences are in a state of constant flux, planners simply do not have an appropriate 'social welfare function' to guide their decisions.

Knowledge is scattered *in the minds* of many dispersed actors, each of whom may possess subjective information that *no one else discerns*. Even in a world of perfect altruism, therefore, public-spirited planners could not obtain the information to engage in a process of conscious social planning owing to the *cognitive limits of the human mind*.[3] In the market economy, by contrast, each entrepreneurial decision actively creates new knowledge that might otherwise have gone unnoticed, and may act to persuade other individuals to change their plans. As competing entrepreneurs and firms make buying and selling decisions, entering and exiting from various markets, the resultant profits and losses may then be noticed by other actors who imitate the behaviour of the successful and learn not to make the same errors as the unsuccessful. As the behaviour of the successful is emulated, more knowledge is produced and spreads throughout the market in a snowballing process, the results of which *could never have been given to a group of minds attempting to simulate this process in advance*.[4] In this manner, the price system brings together the dispersed 'bits' of information divided among the various individuals and firms.

Crucially, it is the *structure of relative resource prices* emerging from a free and open market, and the constant changes in this structure, which facilitate 'economising' behaviour and hence the

---

3   Hayek, 1948, op. cit.
4   ibid.

best use of available resources. In a world where various resource combinations can be put to a multiplicity of different uses, decision-makers must have some ready basis for comparison between alternative courses of action. Without a set of relative resource prices, decision-makers lack the information needed to determine which of all the possible combinations of resource uses should be adopted, that is, those that generate the highest value from the minimum set of inputs.

Market-generated prices, therefore, facilitate economic calculation, but for these prices to be reflective of the changing ideas and behaviour of individuals and firms, it is imperative that they be determined through a process of open competition. This *does not* require the notion of 'perfect competition' inherent in the neoclassical model, where markets with large numbers of 'price-takers' adjust instantaneously. Rather, it simply requires that existing market participants be open to challenge from new entrants offering better opportunities than are currently available. Under these conditions, free-market prices act as surrogates (albeit imperfect ones) for the ideas and actions of dispersed actors. Therefore attempts to set prices by government fiat or to replicate the results of markets (by computer simulations, for example) are doomed to failure since the results that would emanate are unknowable in the absence of *real competition* and the 'social division of knowledge' on which this process draws.

Hayekian political economy is *not*, it should be noted, opposed to the notion of 'planning' per se. On the contrary, the market is viewed as a form of *decentralised social planning* in which the changing plans of dispersed individuals and firms are constantly adjusted to one another through the medium of the price system. Similarly, the Hayekian perspective recognises that there may be important social gains in terms of reducing transaction costs and the benefits-of-scale economies to be made from centralisation and the operation of a hierarchical management system. As Coase famously pointed out, this is, after all, *why firms exist*.[5] It may be that in order to reduce uncertainty and to pool risks, larger, bureaucratic organisations may at times experience a competitive advantage over decentralised units. Market competition is a multipurpose instrument, which can help to discover how much 'planning' there should actually be. The appropriate boundary between the spontaneous order of 'the market' (the realm of the price system) and the planned or designed order of the firm (the realm of organisation/hierarchy) is itself subject to a process of entrepreneurial experimentation. It is for this very reason that the size and number of firms in different sectors vary so markedly from decade to decade.[6] Markets, therefore, while far from 'perfect', may offer a better mechanism for determining the appropriate scale of 'planning organisations' than administration by government bureaucracies, which are not subject to an equivalent competitive discovery procedure.

Government land-use planning and the pretence of knowledge

The Hayekian critique of government planning is, of course, at its most forceful when explaining the failure of attempts to plan the entire economy, but its conclusions also apply to lesser measures

---

5   R. H. Coase, 'The Nature of the Firm', *Economica*, vol. 4, 1937, pp. 386–405.
6   For empirical evidence on these trends, see, Y. Brozen, *Competition, Mergers and Public Policy*, Macmillan, New York, 1982; D. R. Steele, *From Marx to Mises*, Open Court, La Salle, Illinois, 1992.

of government control, especially when these act to suppress the generation of market prices. Applying these arguments to land-use planning suggests, therefore, that it may be a 'pretence of knowledge' to maintain that government land-use controls can 'improve' on apparently haphazard market processes.

Not surprisingly, problems associated with attempts to achieve 'integrated land-use planning' in Britain have been at their most severe the more comprehensive has been the attempt to plan the land-use system as a whole. One of the clearest manifestations of the deficiencies of government planning in this regard was revealed with the failure of the postwar New Towns programme. This particular 'integrated land-use policy' aimed to create a series of 'free-standing' towns, built by the state on green-field sites acquired under compulsory purchase and separated from existing urban areas through a series of Green Belts. The New Towns were designed to accommodate 'excess' population from the older conurbations and were to be 'self-contained', with the bulk of employment and service-provision needs confined within the boundaries of the towns themselves. The purpose of the policy, therefore, was to relieve problems of urban congestion in the older cities, and simultaneously to discourage urban sprawl and the growth of long-distance commuting.

In the event planners' predictions regarding the likely effect of future population/employment growth and the transport pattern effects of the towns proved wildly inaccurate. Population expanded at a much higher rate than was planned for, and the New Towns, far from being 'self-contained', developed into major 'importers' and 'exporters' of population and employment. Some, such as Milton Keynes, became major urban centres, attracting population and employment from elsewhere. Others, such as

Basildon and Hemel Hempstead, became little more than dormitory towns for the London commuter market. Indeed, short of imposing restrictions on freedom of movement resembling those enforced throughout the Soviet bloc, it is difficult to see how the goal of 'self-containment' could ever have been achieved. As a consequence of the inability of planners to adjust effectively to constantly changing circumstances, the New Towns policy persisted long after its original goals had been subverted. The policy may, as a result, have led to greater levels of population decentralisation, urban sprawl and long-distance commuting than if the older urban areas had been allowed to expand outward in a gradual, incremental way.[7]

The experience of New Towns calls clearly into question the notion that government planning is able to correct for the alleged 'short-termism' of private agents and to manage the effects of uncertainty in decision-making. In the marketplace, if the value to future consumers of land in a particular use is greater than it is to those in the present, private property owners may receive a financial signal that provides an incentive to conserve. Because the future is inherently uncertain, subjective considerations are inevitably involved in analysing the future profitability of alternative uses, and it is because of this uncertainty that errors will be made and land markets will be prone to 'failure'. Markets, however, although manifestly imperfect, may allow for a wider range of forecasts to be made, *at least some of which may prove to be accurate*. Government land-use planning, on the other hand, tends to be far less polycentric in its decision-making, and should an error

---

7   J. Simmie, *Planning at the Crossroads*, UCL Press, London, 1993; G. Cherry, *Town Planning in Britain since 1900*, Blackwell, Oxford, 1996.

occur, the negative consequences may, as the New Towns case suggests, be correspondingly more far-reaching.

The planning errors exemplified by New Towns are perhaps in danger of repetition with respect to the current government's desire to formulate more 'integrated land-use policies'. The contemporary planning literature is polarised between advocates of 'compact settlement' approaches (currently in favour with DEFRA) as the best way of tackling problems of urban pollution and congestion[8] and those who favour a more low-density alternative.[9] The former argue that higher-density developments reduce the need for car-based travel and longer commuter or shopping trips. According to this perspective, higher-density developments reduce the need for auto use because people are able to access a wider range of services within a smaller surface area. The latter, by contrast, contend that in certain circumstances higher densities may actually *increase* car use because shorter origin-destination trips reduce the average cost per trip. Cheaper trips may mean *more* vehicle trips so that *total* vehicle-miles travelled may increase in compact settlements. Much-maligned out-of-town shopping developments may, therefore, be less likely to increase pollution than town-centre equivalents. Although people may travel longer distances to the former, the frequency of these visits tends to be less, so it is not at all clear that discriminating

---

8   Report of the Urban Taskforce, *Towards an Urban Renaissance*, E & F Spon, London, 1999.

9   R. Crane, 'Cars and Drivers in the New Suburbs: Linking Access to Travel in neo-Traditional Planning', *Journal of the American Planning Association*, vol. 62, no. 1, 1996, pp. 51–65; P. Gordan and H. W. Richardson, 'Are Compact Cities a Desirable Planning Goal?', *Journal of the American Planning Association*, vol. 63, no. 1, 1997, pp. 95–107; P. Hall, *Sustainable Cities or Town Cramming?*, Town and Country Planning Association, London, 1998.

against such developments will do anything to reduce auto-based pollution.

In practice there would appear to be considerable uncertainty concerning the effect of different urban forms on transit patterns and related levels of pollution. From a Hayekian point of view, *none* of the relevant 'experts' may know the 'optimal' policy response, because the range of interconnected variables that contribute to the quality of urban life may be far too complex to rely on in a conscious attempt to 'integrate' the land-use system. There is so much 'expert' disagreement about the likely effect of different urban forms (high-density versus low-density, etc.) on pollution and congestion levels because there are so many interconnected variables that are difficult to predict or model.

Moreover, as the planning debate itself so clearly illustrates, the environmental costs and benefits of different density developments remain highly subjective. None of the relevant commentators may genuinely be in a position to judge the 'social costs' of different schemes and must instead rely on their own subjective preferences to define what types of development would constitute an improvement in the 'quality of life'. From a Hayekian perspective, the costs and benefits associated with environmental externalities are inherently subjective and are only revealed through the actions and choices that people make when confronted with a range of competing alternatives. The best way of dealing with the relevant uncertainties, therefore, may not be deliberately to plan for an 'optimal' urban form, but to permit a wider variety of *experiments in urban living*. This may allow a discovery process to reveal which particular ways of organising urban areas work best from the *subjective view of their inhabitants* as signalled by the *relative* willingness to pay for different types of development scheme.

The informational problems of government land-use planning discussed above stem primarily from the difficulties of attributing values to a variety of land-use externalities without a competitive market process and the comparative price signals that such a process produces. In the absence of such prices, attempts to create an 'optimal' mix of land uses are likely to be arbitrary, reflecting the subjective valuations of the planners concerned. If such decisions fail to reflect the constantly changing structure of public preferences and individual behaviour patterns, then there is no direct feedback mechanism for the planner comparable to the financial loss and potential for bankruptcy experienced in the market.

Planning without prices: incremental planning

Defenders of government land-use planning and of the British planning system in particular often respond to the above line of criticism by maintaining that the planning system *does*, in fact, involve a significant element of decentralisation and allows scope for local discretion and experimentation in the way that policies are carried out.[10] As was noted earlier, the responsibility for planning decisions in Britain is divided between a variety of agencies at different levels of government, and is closer to a 'mixed-economy' model than to a 'centrally planned' regime. Directed programmes such as New Towns policy have tended to be the exception rather than the rule. In this sense, the experience of planning in Britain has more in common with Lindblom's notion of incrementalism than with comprehensive or 'blueprint' planning schemes.

---

10 See, for example, Report of the Nuffield Foundation, *Town and Country Planning*, the Nuffield Foundation, London, 1986.

To defend the British planning system on the grounds that it is not a centrally planned system is, however, a peculiar line of argument. In truth, there has *never*, in the purest sense of the term, been a centrally planned system operating *anywhere in the modern world*. Even the 'planned economies' of the former Soviet bloc and pre-1979 communist China were forced, out of sheer necessity, to rely on an element of decentralisation owing to the practical impossibility of controlling everything from the centre.[11] In each of these cases responsibility for the implementation and in some cases for the formulation of 'plans' was devolved down to individual factories or to more localised tiers of administration. None of this apparent decentralisation, however, does anything to undermine Hayekian criticisms of such systems. On the contrary, it is the central focus of the Hayekian argument to pose the question of *how* in the *absence of market prices* the actions of such decentralised planning agencies are to be properly co-ordinated or 'integrated' with one another. It was, of course, the very lack of such a mechanism which was responsible for the chronic inability of the 'planned economies' to achieve co-ordination between their component parts.

As Hayek put it:

> ... once decentralisation becomes necessary, the problem of co-ordination arises – a co-ordination which leaves the separate agencies free to adjust their activities to the facts which only they can know and yet brings about a mutual adjustment of their respective plans ... This is precisely what the price system does under competition, and what no other system even promises to accomplish. It enables

---

11   See, for example, P. Craig Roberts, *Alienation and the Soviet Economy*, Holmes and Meir, New York, 1990.

> entrepreneurs, by watching the movements of
> comparatively few prices, as an engineer watches the hands
> of a few dials, to adjust their activities to those of their
> fellows.[12]

It is this very lack of co-ordination resulting from the suppression of the price system which has historically characterised the relationship between the different components of the British land-use planning system. In areas such as development control, the allocation of housing land and the siting of major infrastructure projects, such as roads and airports, there has been a legacy of dis-coordination between the various government agencies concerned. In the case of housing land allocations, for example, inter-agency conflicts are standard fare. There are frequent political battles between DEFRA and individual planning authorities with regard to the number of new housing developments to be permitted within particular counties and districts. It is common for local authorities to ignore the recommendations of DEFRA inspectors and to set their own (usually much lower) housing land allocations, only to have the relevant plans 'called in' by the Secretary of State. Similar inter-agency conflicts occur at the local level, where the disputes between different district authorities and between counties and districts over the location of new housing and other major developments amount to little more than a game of inter-agency 'pass the parcel'.

It is precisely this lack of co-ordination which results in the frequent calls for a more 'joined-up' or 'integrated' planning system, and an end to the 'disjointed incrementalism' of the existing

---

12   Hayek, 1944, op. cit., pp. 55–6.

regime.[13] Such integration is, however, unlikely to be forthcoming in the absence of an effectively functioning price mechanism. Without the market pricing of their activities it will be difficult for the various government agencies to learn how much housing development should be permitted and in which jurisdictions, to discover the appropriate balance between 'brown-' and 'green-field' development, and to decide where major infrastructure projects should be accommodated, and so forth. Moreover, in the absence of open competition there is no obvious mechanism for determining which particular government agencies should be responsible for the relevant planning functions, how many such agencies there should be, and the appropriate balance between centralisation and decentralisation in the system.

None of the above is to say that *no* information is communicated by the existing planning regime and that *no* co-ordination or learning is brought about. Developers, for example, may feed their own specialised knowledge of market conditions and of prices into the plan-making process at public inquiries. Similarly, the different planning departments involved may engage in various interagency forums and consult with environmental groups and other interested parties. These forums, such as the South East Regional Planning Conference (SERPLAN), attempt to determine the amount and type of development to be permitted within a given region and to share this out between the constituent authorities.

Each of these mechanisms may facilitate a degree of learning between the agencies concerned, and an element of mutual adjustment as suggested by the incremental model. From a Hayekian

---

13　See, for example, Report of the Nuffield Foundation, op. cit.; Report of the Urban Taskforce, op. cit.

perspective, however, such mechanisms are a poor substitute for the *fine-grained* adjustments to the constant changes in supply and demand, changing lifestyles and individual preferences that are facilitated by a set of relative prices. In the case of structure and local plans, for example, such documents are typically years out of date by the time of their completion.[14] Without market prices to indicate changes in the *relative* salience of various competing objectives (conservation versus development, for example), and how best to achieve them, it is difficult for the planning agencies involved to compare the merits of alternative courses of action and to adjust their plans accordingly.

Planning without prices: collaborative planning

The informational problems discussed above are unlikely to be addressed simply by increasing levels of public participation in the plan-making process, as argued by the enthusiasts for 'collaborative' planning. Whilst it must surely be accepted that participatory procedures may generate more information than purely 'expert-centred' modes of decision, there are a number of problems with the assumption that a participatory, democratic planning system can deliver an appropriately 'integrated' set of land-use decisions.

First, to suggest that *because* social and environmental systems are 'holistically' related entities they must be managed on a similarly 'holistic' or 'joined-up' basis[15] is a complete *non sequitur*. From a Hayekian perspective it is precisely *because* these systems are *complexly* related entities that *conscious* social planning is

---

14   See, for example, Simmie, op. cit.; Cherry, op. cit.
15   Healey, op. cit.

problematic. Advocates of participatory planning appear to be suggesting that fundamental epistemological problems could somehow be solved if only all the relevant 'stakeholders', in their multiple social and economic roles, could be gathered together in some sort of grand committee meeting to discuss the issues in hand (a logistical impossibility in itself). As both Hayek's work and recent developments in chaos and complexity theory suggest, however, it is because of the *magnitude of the interrelations* between the many components that make up a complex economy that they may *not* be grasped synoptically by a group of minds engaged in such a discussion.[16]

The logistical problems of participatory planning are revealed when one examines the institutional mechanisms that are advocated. It is never suggested that all or even a majority of the relevant populations will be involved in the requisite plan-making. Instead, the devices proposed include 'citizens' juries', 'community workshops' or 'focus groups' – small groups of citizens randomly selected from the populations concerned.[17] When involved in the making of strategic plans and other 'integrated land-use policies', such groups are to make more comprehensible the complex interrelationships that permeate urban and regional economies, which are held to be beyond the comprehension of professional technocracy. For the reasons outlined above, such claims seem questionable. How, for example, are the members of citizens' juries to learn reflexively about the quality of their deci-

---

16   F. A. Hayek, 'The Theory of Complex Phenomena', in *Studies in Philosophy, Politics and Economics*, Routledge, 1967 (a); D. Parker and R. Stacey, *Chaos, Management and Economics: The Implications of Non-Linear Thinking*, Institute of Economic Affairs, London, 1994.

17   Healey, op. cit.

sions when there is no equivalent of the profit-and-loss account and the constant feedback (positive and negative) provided by a set of relative prices which can 'test' the quality of the choices made? Similarly, how are voters to make meaningful judgements on the performance of such processes if the actors concerned are attempting to engage in a process that may be beyond *anybody's* comprehension? One might also ask *why* the population in general should feel the sense of empowerment that is often claimed. It is far from clear why the multitude of people, who cannot for logistical reasons be involved, should feel any more 'empowered' than they might feel under the rule of technocratic procedures.

Given that 'the environment' is *not* an all-or-nothing good, but a bundle of *different* goods, it is hard to see how even relatively simple communication/co-ordination problems could be adequately addressed by the participatory planning approach. To learn, for example, that some members of a citizens' jury would prefer that fewer green-field sites be allocated for house-building, whilst others are prepared to tolerate the further loss of such sites, is to learn very little at all. How few is fewer? How do the environmental costs of building houses vary from one green-field site to another? For what combination of purposes are green-field sites to be used? Such questions will, of course, be multiplied many times over when the choice is between the vast array of potential land uses that make up a complex economy, the myriad possible combinations of such uses and the complexity of their environmental consequences. In short, without the information provided by a set of market-generated *relative prices* it will be difficult for participants, in other than the crudest form, to communicate their values to each other, and hence to find ways of 'integrating' these values with those of their fellows.

Land use and tacit knowledge

The problems discussed above with regard to the incremental and collaborative planning models are encapsulated in the inability of these institutions to transform what Hayek and Polanyi termed 'tacit knowledge' into a socially usable form.[18] Tacit knowledge may include such things as 'on the job knowhow', 'local knowledge' or the capacity to 'know a particular market'. In addition, tacit knowledge may also include an individual's personal knowledge of the kinds of things he or she wants and values, the precise differences in which may not, however, be conveyed explicitly in verbal form.

From a Hayekian perspective, the virtue of the market is that it is able to translate such knowledge of local conditions and values, which cannot be articulated, into a readily usable form via the structure of relative prices that emerges unintentionally from competitive acts of buying and selling. As Buchanan observed, 'cost' can only be dated 'at the moment of choice', that is, when people are faced with a real decision and must choose between available alternatives.[19] When people make buying and selling decisions in markets, as producers (choosing which goods to pro-

---

18 Hayek, 1948, op. cit.; M. Polanyi, *The Logic of Liberty*, University of Chicago Press, Chicago, 1951.

19 J. M. Buchanan, *Cost and Choice*, University of Chicago Press, Chicago, 1969. It is, of course, for this reason that 'contingent valuation' and other survey-based methods of environmental evaluation proposed by welfare economists such as Pearce *et al.* (1989) are inappropriate. Such surveys pose a set of *hypothetical* scenarios asking people what they *would* do or what they *would* be willing to pay *if* they were faced with a choice of protecting a particular environmental asset. Since the actors concerned are not required to make a *real* choice, the necessary tacit knowledge of how they value one good in relation to another is unlikely to be revealed by such techniques – even granting that those conducting the survey could accurately predict what the appropriate choice scenario might be.

duce and how to produce them), and as consumers (choosing between a variety of purchasing alternatives), they transmit 'messages' to others about how much they value a particular course of action. Prices, therefore, serve as a subtle communication medium, making the private and often tacit knowledge of individuals available in a form that others can readily access and adjust to.

In the case of land-use planning, different parcels of land have a myriad of potential uses, so for land to be put to its most valued use there must be a mechanism that can transform knowledge of competing demands (such as housing, recreation and conservation) into a form that can easily be deciphered by others. From a Hayekian perspective, bargaining in markets may be sensitive to variations in local conditions, with the parties to an exchange more likely to possess the relevant information 'on the ground'. The different prices that emerge from such exchanges may then transmit information about local variations in environmental quality/competing pressures on land use to more distant actors who may adjust their own behaviour accordingly – shifting development pressure from more environmentally sensitive and hence more expensive sites, for example. Alternative models of planning, by contrast, including those that emphasise a role for public participation, lack the capacity to transform such tacit knowledge into an accessible form. While some information of this type may be transmitted by verbal means, there is a larger body of such knowledge which *cannot* be communicated linguistically. Public inquiries and interest-group politics, for example, are less able to convey the *relative* significance of different uses of land when compared to the *fine-grained* differences and comparisons of value attached to various land parcels which may be expressed through the price system.

The perverse effects that can flow from the inability of government planning institutions to communicate tacit knowledge effectively are well demonstrated by the experience of the 'jewel' in the
British planning crown – Green Belt policy. At present, approxim-
ately 14 per cent of the land area of England is covered by this particular statutory designation, which forbids most forms of
development in large swathes of land around the major towns and
cities in an attempt to stop the outward growth of the larger urban
areas.[20] As such, Green Belts suffer from many of the deficiencies
of similar 'command-and-control' regulations. The principal difficulty is that, as a blanket ban on development, Green Belts pay virtually no attention to local variations in environmental quality
within the designated land.

It is rarely acknowledged that the level of environmental quality within Green Belts *varies dramatically*. The London Green Belt,
for example, whilst including the wooded hills of the Chilterns and
the North Downs, also includes huge tracts of land on the western
and eastern urban fringes, consisting of disused gravel pits, quar-
ries, railway and motorway embankments and low-grade farm-
land/horticultural developments. While there is clearly a public
desire to preserve aesthetically attractive sites within easy reach of
the city, it is equally the case that many people currently struggling
to find access to affordable housing might be prepared to see the
relatively less attractive parts of the Green Belt developed for residential purposes.

Indeed, in many areas within the boundaries of the Green Belt
itself, well-designed and landscaped housing developments, sur-

---

20 B. Cullingworth and V. Nadin, *Town and Country Planning in Britain*, Routledge,
London, 1997.

rounded by, say, newly planted woodlands, might well constitute an environmental improvement. This argument is especially pertinent when considering that for every site of doubtful environmental quality preserved within the Green Belt itself, pressure mounts for the development of potentially *more attractive and more valued* sites in the rural areas *beyond* the designated zones. When taking into account the level of development that has been displaced into the 'deep countryside' rather than taking place on the immediate urban fringe, Green Belts may have resulted in a *greater loss* of valued rural sites than might otherwise have been the case.[21]

Supporters of the Green Belt argue that the purpose of the policy has never been to protect the aesthetic qualities of the countryside as such, but to prevent the merging of urban areas to form contiguous stretches of 'sprawl' in which the identity of previously distinct communities is submerged into a homogeneous urban mass. These arguments are not without merit, but again the assumption underlying Green Belt policy is that such issues arise with the same force at all times and in all places. The importance attached to maintaining distinct boundaries to towns and villages is, however, likely to vary considerably from place to place depending on the specific location, environmental characteristics and history of the community concerned. A blanket command-and-control policy such as the Green Belt is incapable of responding to the diversity of local conditions that exists and hence may lead to what are potentially worse environmental outcomes overall. Without being guided by a set of relative prices, which can highlight variations in environmental quality between different

---

21 Simmie, op. cit. See also J. Herington, *The Outer City*, Paul Chapman, London, 1984; J. Herington, *Green Belts*, Regional Studies Association/Jessica Kingsley, London, 1990.

parcels of land, planners are less able to allocate planning permissions to the most appropriate uses.

Land use and spontaneous order

Seen through a Hayekian lens, the myriad interdependencies that link the patchwork of land uses of both urban and rural environments are classic examples of spontaneous social and economic orders, the complexities of which cannot be overseen synoptically. As Jane Jacobs' work demonstrates so well, the fundamentally human character of land-use processes makes the form, pattern and pace of development unpredictable and beyond the scope of planners, whether technocratic experts or members of citizens' juries.[22] Land-use systems involve dynamic processes that are connected to subjective human purposes yet are at the same time evolving beyond anybody's comprehension. They are, as Hayek, following Adam Ferguson, memorably put it, 'the result of human action, but not of human design'.[23]

Consequently, rather than seeking to manage the land-use system according to some holistic plan, it may be better to rely on *self-organising mechanisms* to bring about the necessary co-ordination.[24] As Di Zerega points out, self-organisation refers to those non-reductionist processes wherein relatively simple reactions by the components of a system result in complex patterns of order far beyond the capacity of each of the component parts to

22   See, for example, J. Jacobs, *The Economy of Cities*, Random House, New York, 1969.

23   F. A. Hayek, 'The Results of Human Action but Not of Human Design', in *Studies in Philosophy, Politics and Economics*, Routledge, London, 1967 (b).

24   Hayek, 1967 (b), op. cit.; Parker and Stacey, op. cit.

construct mechanically. Such orders arise where the individual participants are involved in co-ordinative processes, the patterns of which *are far too complex for them to grasp.*[25]

The price-guided market may, therefore, be a more appropriate mechanism for co-ordinating a complex land-use system than the notion of 'integrated land-use planning'. The constant process of feedback provided by the changing structure of *relative prices* within the market brings together dispersed knowledge and facilitates a degree of mutual adjustment and co-ordination that may be greater than could be achieved if those concerned had sought to plan the outcome in advance. The most that can be understood about such spontaneous orders are the *general* principles (such as the tendency for prices to rise when demand exceeds supply) that connect the multitude of component parts. How *specific* individual acts of co-ordination will come about, however, may never be known in sufficient detail.[26] This is not to argue that markets provide a perfect mechanism for co-ordinating land uses, but at the very least the Hayekian perspective suggests that due attention should be given to the informational disadvantages of government land-use planning and the advantages of relying on decentralised market discovery processes.

---

25   G. Di Zerega, 'Social Ecology, Deep Ecology and Liberalism', *Critical Review*, vol. 6, nos 2–3, 1993, pp. 305–70.

26   Hayek, op. cit., 1967 (a) and (b); Di Zerega, op. cit.

4 PUBLIC-CHOICE OBJECTIONS TO GOVERNMENT LAND-USE PLANNING[1]

The analysis thus far has concentrated on the informational deficiencies of government land-use planning when compared to market processes. None of these arguments has sought to call into question the motivations of the planners and 'stakeholders' involved in the relevant decision-making. On the contrary, the power of the Hayekian critique stems in large part from the fact that it *does not* challenge the assumption that those involved in the process of planning may act or may think they are acting on the basis of achieving the 'public interest'. Rather, the analysis points to the insurmountable 'knowledge problems' of utilising information with regard to individual preferences, relative resource scarcities and local environmental conditions, which are dispersed throughout society.

When taking into account Hayekian arguments, the seemingly overwhelming case for government land-use regulation looks considerably weaker. The case for planning looks weaker still, however, if the assumption that planners are motivated *solely* with regard to the public interest is relaxed. If we heed Adam Smith's dictum that rarely does anything of merit come from those who

---

1   The arguments set out in this section are a summary of a much lengthier and more detailed empirical analysis of public-choice processes in the British planning system – see M. Pennington, *Planning and the Political Market: Public Choice and the Politics of Government Failure*, Athlone Press, London, 2000.

claim to 'trade for the public good', then the possibility arises that planners and 'stakeholding' interest groups may be motivated, in part at least, by their own *self-interest*. In these circumstances, attention should turn to an examination of *incentive structures* facing the actors in the planning process and the extent to which the institutions of the planning system are likely to channel these incentives in line with the preferences of the populace at large. It is at this point, therefore, that we should consider the 'public choice' problems involved in government land-use planning.

Rational ignorance and special-interest capture

From a public-choice perspective, a primary institutional defect in collective government decision-making stems from the insufficient incentive which voters may have to monitor the performance of their elected representatives.[2] Because the costs of acquiring accurate political information are very high, compared to the minuscule influence each individual is likely to have on the result of an election, it may be rational for voters to remain ignorant of the political process.[3] This rational-ignorance effect

---

2   There are, of course, principal agent/incentive problems in the private sector, which stem from the separation of ownership and control following the development of the modern capitalist corporation. In the private sector, however, even where shareholders can have little effect on the day-to-day process of management, they are able to exert indirect control on management performance by observing stock prices and by exercising their right to sell their shares and to invest elsewhere. In the public sector, by contrast, individuals do not own shares that can be bought and sold, so there may be relatively less opportunity, *even indirectly*, for members of the public to discipline poor management performance.

3   See, for example, G. Tullock, *The Economics of Special Privilege and Rent Seeking*, Kluwer Academic Press, London, 1989; G. Tullock, *Rent Seeking*, Edward Elgar, Aldershot, 1993.

may account for the failure of many members of the electorate to know even the name of their own MP, let alone the detailed effects of legislation. Consumers choosing in the private marketplace, by contrast, have a much greater incentive to acquire information because the costs of any purchasing errors will be concentrated on the individuals concerned. It is this propensity towards rational ignorance when individuals act as voters as opposed to private consumers which frequently allows the political process to be 'captured' by special-interest groups or 'rent-seekers'.

In public-choice theory, a special-interest issue is defined as one that generates substantial personal benefits for a relatively small number of constituents, while simultaneously imposing a small individual cost on a much larger, *unidentified* group of voters. Politicians, eager to maintain popularity and ultimately to ensure re-election, may 'supply' legislation that concentrates benefits on special-interest groups and may attempt to win elections by putting together majority coalitions of such groups. Although the gains to the special interests may be outweighed by losses to the populace at large, the latter are unlikely to mobilise because the numbers concerned are of such an order that the likelihood of an individual contribution being decisive to the success of the group is minuscule.

As a consequence, the political process is likely to be skewed in favour of smaller, more concentrated groups (such as producer interests), at the expense of larger, more diffuse constituencies (such as consumer interests).[4] Such incentives are, it should be noted, *structural* deficiencies *inherent* in political decision-making proce-

---

4   M. Olson, *The Logic of Collective Action*, Harvard University Press, 1965; M. Olson, *The Rise and Decline of Nations*, Yale University Press, 1982; W. Mitchell and R. Simmons, *Beyond Politics*, Westview Press, Boulder, 1994.

dures and are unlikely to be addressed, on other than the most superficial level, by opening up the policy process to greater levels of public participation. Indeed, providing additional opportunities for such participation may only be successful in providing additional opportunities for special-interest access at the expense of diffuse interests that remain chronically under-mobilised within the political process.

Rational ignorance and special-interest capture in British planning

The combined effects of rational voter ignorance and special-interest capture are well illustrated in British land-use planning. The chronic information deficit facing the electorate is notably apparent in terms of public perceptions of the land-use problems faced. This is especially so in terms of rural to urban land ratios, and hence of the perceived need to protect 'green-field' sites 'at any cost'. Evidence suggests that public opinion is, to say the least, ill informed with regard to the degree of urbanisation. As Cullingworth notes, survey evidence indicates that two-thirds of the electorate believe that 65 per cent or more of the UK surface area is devoted to urban land uses, such as roads and housing, when the actual figure is a mere 11 per cent.[5] Similar information problems appear also to underwrite the widespread perception in the media and among the public at large that the 1980s were a decade of *deregulation* characterised by unprecedented rates of green-field development. In fact, of over two hundred proposals

---

5   B. Cullingworth, *Town and Country Planning in Britain*, 10th ed., Routledge, London, 1988, p. 184.

put forward for 'new settlements' in the countryside in the mid to late 1980s, only seven were granted planning permission. Overall, the 1980s witnessed *the lowest rate of rural to urban land conversion of any decade since the interwar period* – a mere 5,000 hectares of land conversion, compared to 15,000 hectares in the 1950s, 15,000 hectares in the 1960s and 10,000 hectares in the 1970s.[6]

Special-interest groups operating within the planning system have been quick to exploit the rational ignorance effect to consolidate their own political power. Foremost among these has been the local amenity lobby epitomised by the Council for the Protection of Rural England (CPRE). Such groups are keen to prevent *any* development from taking place 'in their backyard' and have been particularly successful in stopping new housing developments in high demand areas such as South-East England. Evidence from the local planning process suggests that over 60 per cent of the changes brought about by the process of public participation result in a reduction in the amount of development proposed as against a mere 13 per cent where development targets are increased.[7] These processes are especially pronounced within designated Green Belts and Areas of Outstanding Natural Beauty (AONBs), where between 90 and 100 per cent of all development applications are refused.

The principal effect of such restrictions has been the inexorable rise in the price of housing land and hence house prices brought about by the increased scarcity of supply. While there is continuing academic debate as to the precise magnitude of the price rises that may be attributed to such nimbyist action, that

6   Cullingworth and Nadin, op. cit.
7   D. Adams, *The Urban Development Process*, Methuen, London, 1995.

prices have risen as a consequence is in little doubt.[8] As land prices have risen, developers have in turn responded to the increased scarcity of supply by cramming as many houses as possible onto the remaining sites in the countryside and the market towns that are granted planning permission. This 'rabbit hutches on postage stamps'[9] syndrome is the proximate cause of the high-density suburban estates characterised by poor architectural quality and a lack of garden space which periodically spring up on the outskirts of towns. As public-choice theory would suggest, however, the consumers who might benefit from a relaxation of restrictions on development, a subsequent fall in prices and an improvement in design standards are lacking effective representation in the planning system because they do not constitute an identifiable, site-specific group that can readily be mobilised. Incentive structures

8   Cheshire and Sheppard use econometric techniques to compare the relatively more relaxed planning regime in Darlington with the more restrictive arrangements in Reading. Their results suggested that housing costs in Reading would be 12 per cent lower in the town centre and 4 per cent lower in the suburbs if the more relaxed policies were introduced. See P. Cheshire and S. Sheppard, *The Welfare Economics of Land Use Regulation*, Research Papers in Environmental and Spatial Analysis, Department of Geography and Environment, London School of Economics and Political Science, 1997.

    Bramley *et al.* (1995) suggest in their econometric model, however, that a relaxation of Green Belts would result in only a 2–3 per cent reduction in housing costs across South East England. According to this analysis, if planning controls were relaxed substantially this would not necessarily result in significantly cheaper house prices because consumers would respond to lower prices by consuming more land which would in turn force up the cost of housing units. See G. Bramley *et al.* (1995), *Planning, the Market and Private Housebuilding*, London: UCL Press. For a critique of Bramley *et al.*'s econometrics on grounds that they understate the price effects of land-use planning, see A. Evans (1996), 'The Impact of Land Use Planning and Tax Subsidies on the Supply and Price of Housing in Britain: A Comment', *Urban Studies*, vol. 33, no. 3, pp. 581–5.

9   A. Evans, 'Rabbit Hutches on Postage Stamps: Planning Development and Political Economy', *Urban Studies*, vol. 28, no. 6, 1991, pp. 853–70.

within the planning system, therefore, point distinctly in the direction of an *anti-development bias*.

To highlight examples of nimbyism in the planning system and their resultant effects is not, it should be emphasised, to call into question the morality of the individuals concerned. On the contrary, the opposition exhibited to new development by those currently living in the vicinity of green-field sites is entirely understandable *given the pattern of incentives* that members of these groups face. It is as a direct consequence of the nationalisation of development rights that people are placed in a position where they have *everything to lose* in terms of amenity and property values and *nothing to gain* in terms of financial compensation when decisions regarding the allocation of housing land and other developments are made. Since the allocation of development rights resides with local planning authorities and ultimately the Secretary of State, communities are faced with an all-or-nothing situation where new development is simply imposed upon them via the discretionary power of the local planning authority or by DEFRA.

The local amenity lobby is not the only set of special interests to have benefited from the operation of the planning system. Evidence suggests that the corporate house-builders have also been important beneficiaries. The granting of planning permission confers a *monopoly right* on developers as other potential development sites are effectively excluded from the market. In accordance with Stigler's economic theory of regulation, therefore, the larger corporate developers prefer a controlled system providing permission to develop their own land while restricting access to development land for potential competitors.[10] It is probably for

---

10   G. Stigler, *The Citizen and the State*, Chicago University Press, Chicago, 1975.

this reason that the planning system tends to operate on the basis of the occasional 'drip-feed' of a few large sites contained within the portfolios of corporate developers, rather than the release of a much larger number of smaller plots owned by the smaller house-building concerns.[11]

More recently, the use of the planning system for collusive purposes has been evidenced in the actions of the larger supermarket chains. Having already built a substantial number of edge-of-town or out-of-town shopping centres throughout the 1980s, the British corporate retailers have put up little opposition to new government restrictions designed to bring a halt to such developments. Indeed, as the opportunities that this regulation affords to restrict entry into the food retail market, and in particular to keep out foreign-owned concerns (such as Walmart, for example) have become apparent, British retail firms have increasingly begun to support such planning measures.[12] It is unfortunate, therefore, that recent media and populist political campaigns against the so-called 'rip-off Britain' syndrome have argued for further regulatory intervention to bring retail prices into line with those in France and in continental Europe as a whole. Evidence suggests that by far the greatest source of retail price differentials between Britain and France is the *relative lack of retail outlets in this country* brought about by the more restrictive planning regime.[13]

The combined effects of such rent-seeking behaviour within

---

11 See, for example, Y. Rydin, *Housing Land Policy*, Gower, Aldershot, 1986; A. Evans, *No Room! No Room!*, Institute of Economic Affairs, London, 1988; Evans, 1991, op. cit.

12 T. Burke and J. Shackleton, *Trouble in Store: UK Retailing in the 1990s*, Hobart Paper 130, Institute of Economic Affairs, London, 1996.

13 Evans, 1988, op. cit.; Mckinsey Global Institute, *Driving Productivity and Growth in the UK Economy*, Mckinsey, London, 1998.

the planning system should not be underestimated. A recent report by the Mckinsey Global Institute supervised by economists not known for their sympathy to market liberalism[14] highlighted the scale of the regulatory costs associated with the current regime. According to this report, while Britain has fared well in relation to its European partners by removing restrictive practices in labour and capital markets, regulatory costs associated with land-use planning are considerably higher in the UK than in much of continental Europe. In turn, the authors argue that such costs are a primary explanatory factor accounting for the relatively poor productivity of a range of sectors across the British economy. In the retail sector, for example, large stores with modern 'hypermarket' formats are by far the most productive outlets. In the UK, however, largely because of planning restrictions, the extent to which such outlets have been allowed to replace the smaller traditional stores has been far smaller than in Europe as a whole. Even the larger stores that are actually built are small by international standards. In France, for example, the average supermarket is typically 50 per cent bigger than its UK equivalent.[15]

Other sectors of the economy have been similarly constrained. According to the Mckinsey authors, in the tourism sector the combination of land-use and building regulations means that the cost of building or refurbishing a hotel is 40 per cent higher than in the United States and France. As a consequence new entry into the hotel market has been severely limited, leaving the country with a stock of outdated hotels (almost 50 per cent of UK hotels are over

14   Mckinsey, op. cit. The steering group of this report was chaired by Professor Robert Solow of the Massachusetts Institute of Technology and included Professor Stephen Nickell of the London School of Economics and Political Science.

15   Mckinsey, op. cit., pp. 13–14.

100 years old, compared to 14 per cent in France) less able to support efficient working practices.[16] Even within relatively high-productivity sectors, such as information technology, the British planning system has imposed substantial constraints. In software, for example, international experience indicates the considerable benefits to be gained from the clustering together of many small entrepreneurial ventures as in Silicon Valley. The development of such clusters in Britain in places such as Oxford and Cambridge has, however, been slowed or even prevented by planning restrictions.[17]

Short-termism and bureaucratic expansionism

Institutional defects within the planning process are not confined to the 'rent-seeking' activities of special-interest groups. Public-choice theory also highlights 'government failures', which may arise from the time horizon of politicians and from the monopoly function of the planning bureaucracy itself. In the former instance, a primary motivation of the politician is the desire to secure re-election, which requires the pursuit of votes. As a result, the political time horizon is unlikely to extend significantly beyond the next election, and there may be little incentive to develop policies the benefits of which may accrue when the originating administration is long gone and a different party may be in power.[18]

The bureaucratic agencies responsible for policy delivery, meanwhile, have interests of their own, which provide additional

---

16   ibid, pp. 14–15.
17   ibid, p. 16.
18   See, for example, G. Tullock, *The Vote Motive*, Institute of Economic Affairs, London, 1977.

potential for 'government failure'. Because planners do not hold private property rights in the resources they control, they cannot capture the benefits or bear the costs of their decisions, so they may not have the same incentives as profit-making firms to allocate resources on the basis of economic or environmental success. Rather, the success of the bureaucrat may be measured in terms of increasing control over discretionary resources, which are often dependent on the size of the agency budget. Bureaucrats, therefore, may have strong incentives to support those policies and interest groups that will expand the size of the bureaucracy and may be aided in their pursuit of resources by the absence of competitive forces within the public sector which would have revealed more efficient production processes.[19]

Short-termism and bureaucratic expansionism in British planning

That the land-use planning system has been subject to the vagaries of short-termist behaviour brought about by politicians' desire to secure immediate popularity is well demonstrated by the experience of the development control procedure and the regular furore surrounding government forecasts of the future demand for housing land. Decisions with regard to the location of new housing development are taken by politicians concerned about the *short-term* impact on their *own constituents*, and not according to the *future benefits* available to the *wider community living outside the area concerned*. The resultant short-termism has been illustrated very

---

19 W. Niskanen, *Bureaucracy and Public Economics*, Edward Elgar, London, 1995; A. Peacock, 'X-Inefficiency: Informational and Institutional Constraints', in H. Hanusch (ed.), *Anatomy of Government Deficiencies*, Springer, Berlin, 1983.

clearly in the recent past by the actions of over two hundred MPs drawn predominantly from market towns and rural marginals, lobbying successfully for a reduction in the predicted requirement of 4.4 million new homes in the next twenty years down to 3.8 million.[20] The relevant DETR (now DEFRA) forecasts are themselves, it should be noted, largely an exercise in short-term political manipulation. The best judges of the future demand for new housing are the developers who operate in the relevant local markets on a daily basis and who possess the necessary tacit knowledge of market conditions. They are the actors who stand to lose money should their forecasts be misjudged. The process of government forecasting appears, therefore, to exist purely as a means of managing short-term opposition to development, especially on greenfield sites. If *actual* development pressure at the local level *outstrips* national government targets, then planning permissions can be refused on the grounds that ' local housing needs', *as defined by national government forecasters*, have already been met!

Turning to the planning bureaucracy itself, there is considerable evidence to support the view that incentives within planning departments point towards a continual process of bureaucratic and regulatory expansion. Between 1962 and 1992 real expenditure on town and country planning in England and Wales increased by over 600 per cent, from £160 million to £1.2 billion (1990 prices) – a rate of increase three times the rate of real growth in the economy over the same period.[21] Neither does it seem that expenditure increases of this magnitude have been matched by improvements in the productivity of the relevant planning

---

20   *The Times*, 26 January 1998.
21   M. Pennington, 'Budgets, Bureaucrats and the Containment of Urban England', *Environmental Politics*, vol. 6, no. 4, 1997 (b), pp. 76–107.

departments. While total real spending on planning increased by over 600 per cent between the 1960s and 1990s, the number of development applications processed by planners increased by a mere 28 per cent over the same period. The difference between these figures must be accounted for, at least in part, by the increasing bureaucratisation of the planning system and a lengthening of the regulatory process, such as the time taken to draw up structure and local plans – now up to four years. It would appear, therefore, that land-use planners have engaged in a process of rapid cost escalation. Planning and development control statistics indicate that the net cost per capita of processing planning applications increased by 85 per cent during the 1980s – the supposed heyday of deregulation. Similarly, current estimates suggest that the productivity rate for local planning departments is a mere two applications processed per month per worker.[22]

The dominant role of centrally raised taxation in the financing of British local government may be a key factor in explaining this continual tendency towards regulatory growth. Where the delivery of local services such as education and policing is dependent on the receipt of *locally raised finance*, then politicians may have an incentive to favour a less tightly controlled system, minimising unnecessary regulation in order to finance service provision and to keep tax

---

22 See Pennington, 1997 (b), op. cit., and Pennington, 2000, op. cit., chapters 4 and 6. The introduction of direct charges for planning applications in the 1980s made little impact on this process since the delivery of the planning service remained a state monopoly and there was little attempt to introduce even minor reforms such as competitive tendering into the planning function. The figure of two applications processed per month per worker actually *overestimates* the productivity rate in local authority planning departments since the vast majority of the applications that are dealt with are for relatively trivial proposals such as the construction of porches and other home extensions.

rates down. As the experience of 'fiscal federalism' in the United States has revealed, this may be an especially pertinent restraint where the population is highly mobile and where the so-called 'Tiebout effect' comes into play.[23] Under these conditions, politicians who fail to allow sufficient development, and as a result raise taxes, face the threat of lost population and revenues as local taxpayers 'shop around' between localities according to the balance of services provided and the taxes charged. *The higher the proportion of central funding, however, the weaker the link between the level of local economic development and the provision of local services and associated tax rates.* In this situation, local politicians can lobby for increased central government transfer payments to make up for any deficit. Seen from this perspective, the reliance of British local authorities on central government transfers (80 per cent of local revenues) may be reducing the incentive for politicians to keep a downward check on the expansionist tendencies within local planning departments.

The growth and enforcement of regulatory controls within the British land-use planning system has, it would seem, been exercised in large part according to special-interest control and bureaucratic discretion. Rather than the process of mutual adjustment to changing circumstances envisaged by incrementalist planning models, or the widespread empowerment of citizens via the extension of public participation, the reality of land-use planning in Britain has often been one of institutional sclerosis and special-interest capture. Benefits have been concentrated on interest groups and bureaucrats with costs dispersed across an invisible mass of taxpayers and consumers.

---

23 C. Tiebout, 'A Pure Theory of Local Expenditures', *Journal of Political Economy*, vol. 64, 1957, pp. 416–24; V. Ostrom *et al.*, *Local Government in the United States*, Institute for Contemporary Studies, San Francisco, 1988.

5 REFORMING LAND-USE PLANNING

The Hayekian and public-choice objections to government land-use planning point to serious institutional deficiencies associated with centralisation, chronic lack of information, the absence of experimentation, and inappropriate incentive structures within the British planning system. What, then, are the institutional alternatives to the current system of land-use control which might help to decentralise decision-making, increase the flow of information, encourage experimentation, and provide a more appropriate set of incentives?

Most proposals for reform of land-use planning accept the basic need for a government-administered system of regulation, and seek an improvement in the quality of decision-making by reforming the system *from within*. Two particular suggestions that often attract attention involve either a move to decentralise all planning functions down to the local government level and/or the greater use of 'market-based' instruments in land-use policy. As will be noted below, both of these suggestions may offer considerable advantages over the present institutional regime. In the final analysis, however, it is the contention of this paper that they are still prone to deficiencies that may be inherent to *any* system of government land-use planning. Having sketched out the essentials of the case for such mechanisms, therefore, the subsequent sections will advance the case for a fundamental *replacement* of government land-use regulation with a more radical denationalisation of decision-making through the creation of private property rights at both the individual and community level.

Local government and the reform of land-use planning

Especially popular with the supporters of 'collaborative' or participatory planning is the idea of devolving most, if not all, land-use planning functions down to the local authority level.[1] According to this perspective, local authorities are much more likely to have access to important 'on the ground' knowledge with regard to such matters as environmental quality and the demand for new housing than are civil servants and ministers. If planning powers were more decentralised, so the argument goes, then decisions would be taken on a basis more reflective of the need to balance different economic and environmental objectives as appropriate to the local situation concerned.

Shifting to a model of land-use planning based entirely at the local government tier would have much to commend it and would undoubtedly avoid many pitfalls of the present more centralised planning regime. Local authority planners *do* exercise a considerable degree of discretion within the existing British planning system, but are continually circumscribed by the need to conform to national policy guidelines. These include Planning Policy Guidance Notes issued by DEFRA, national projections of the demand for housing land, regionally based targets for the accommodation of this demand, and national policies with regard to statutory designations such as the Green Belt. It is not too much

---

1   Healey, op. cit.

of an exaggeration to suggest that this particular model of decision-making is positively Soviet in inspiration. Central government housing demand projections cannot possibly hope to be sensitive to the complex variations in the structure and composition of demand that can only be revealed in the relevant local markets. Similarly, national land-use designations such as the Green Belt are chronically lacking in sensitivity to local variations in environmental quality *within* the designated zones.

The curtailment of national-level planning powers, therefore, and the further decentralisation of power down to the local authority level, might help to make the regulatory system more flexible and sensitive to local economic and environmental conditions. Where the local desire for economic growth is thought to outweigh conservation objectives, then local authorities would have the freedom to introduce more relaxed planning policies. Likewise, where local conservation objectives outweigh economic development, then a more stringent planning regime might be required. Central planning institutions are simply not in a position to comprehend the complexity of land-use systems at the local level and the interrelationships that exist between different localities. It is doubtful, therefore, whether there is *any* need for a 'national land-use strategy' or for any national planning guidelines at all. 'Strategic' planning decisions, such as the siting of major roads and other public infrastructure, which have implications beyond the confines of any single local authority jurisdiction may be better dealt with through 'inter-authority' bargaining organised through bodies such as SERPLAN. Devolving power away from the DEFRA could only act to improve the system by removing what is arguably an unnecessary layer of central government bureaucracy.

Notwithstanding the improvements that would be brought

about by a localised planning system, these are unlikely to be of a sufficient order unless combined with other, more fundamental reforms. Empowering local actors to take decisions can be very beneficial, *but only if these actors are faced with an incentive structure that encourages them to weigh costs and benefits and to be properly accountable for the relevant decisions.* Under the existing planning system, local authorities and their constituents may have environmental externalities associated with inappropriate private development effectively imposed on them from above by organisations such as DEFRA. Equally, however, in many situations local authorities are themselves not held sufficiently to account for the *externalities attached to their own actions*. Locally empowered groupings that seek to block any new development in 'their backyard' also impose costs on the rest of society, especially in terms of higher house prices and increasingly congested urban living environments. At present, however, there are few incentives for local politicians to resist pressure from such nimbyist interests because Whitehall will provide subsidies in order to make up for the lost business and tax revenues associated with over-regulation. It is for precisely this reason that there would appear to be such a pronounced anti-development bias within the British planning system.

A more localised planning system would need, therefore, to be matched with a return to a system of locally raised taxation so as to reintroduce the 'Tiebout effect' into the local government function. Local authorities and their constituents would be more likely to weigh the costs and benefits of new development to the wider community if they were held financially accountable for their decisions. If new development is prohibited, then politicians and their constituents will have to consider the higher local taxes that might be required to fund better local services as a result. In this situation local people will be given more of an incentive to consider the appropriate trade-offs between economic development and environmental protection than is the case under the existing regime. In addition, the increased competition that would ensue with the onset of Tiebout forces would encourage a greater diversity of land-use policies, as local authorities would need to compete to attract potential residents by offering different packages of local services – including land-use and environmental policies – in order to secure a tax base. Concerns over inequalities that may emerge between more affluent areas and those with a less substantial tax base would be better addressed by redistributing resources *directly to low-income people*. Giving people money to spend *themselves* is much more likely to create a sense of 'empowerment' than having the relevant resources spent by government bureaucracies, be they national or local.

The reintroduction of the Tiebout effect into British local government would not, however, act to cure all of the ills associated with the present planning regime. On the one hand, nimbyist interests might continue to wield a disproportionate influence under such a system, so long as those negatively affected by development proposals are unable to obtain some form of direct financial compensation. If development rights continue to be vested in the state, albeit at the local authority level, then the scope for bargaining between the parties to a planning dispute will remain severely limited. There is always likely to remain a danger that over-regulation will prevail in this situation, and with it the possibility that local authorities might transform themselves into 'demand-side' interest groups lobbying for financial intervention from central government, should they start to lose local tax revenues.

A still more fundamental objection to a Tiebout-based strategy of reform, however, is that the entire approach rests on the assumption that local authorities are the appropriate jurisdictional level to engage in effective land-use planning. In an open market, if a firm becomes too large/hierarchical and is unable to make sufficient use of the price system to determine internal resource allocation, then it may be vulnerable to smaller, more flexible competitors better able to access information about changing relative scarcities and market conditions. Whilst economies of scale and the capacity to pool risks/reduce uncertainty may be an advantage of larger organisations, such organisations may also be subject to countervailing inefficiencies. Open competition in the market provides a useful way of testing out a variety of organisational forms and of deciding the appropriate costs and benefits associated with differing levels of centralisation/decentralisation.

Local government planners, however, are not subject to entry from new organisations. In many cases, local authority boundaries have effectively been imposed on communities in an arbitrary way, and for political reasons that have little to do with their efficacy in delivering local services and improving environmental quality. It is, for example, far from clear that decisions over the location of new housing developments should be made by a county council, or a district council, as opposed to a parish council, or even at the level of an individual street or neighbourhood. Local government planning is predicated on the suspension of competitive forces from below, and thus eliminates the very sort of Hayekian discovery procedure that may be necessary to determine the appropriate level at which land-use planning should actually take place.

'Market-based' policy tools and reform of land-use planning

Partly as a recognition of the difficulties with orthodox modes of land-use regulation, whether at the national or local scale, a further strategy for reforming the planning system has been the greater use of so-called 'market-based' policy instruments. As in other fields of environmental policy, 'market-based' policy tools are held to avoid some of the problems of orthodox 'command-and-control' regulations because they are designed to provide people with better incentives and allow a greater element of flexibility in the manner in which environmental goals can be achieved. The policy instruments that have attracted the greatest attention from a land-use planning point of view have been the use of tradable permit schemes[2] and the possibility of 'auctioning' development rights.[3]

Tradable permits

The benefits to be derived from tradable permits with regard to reduced bureaucracy and incentives to higher standards in areas such as atmospheric pollution control are now well documented.[4] Under tradable pollution permits the government sets the level of atmospheric emissions to be tolerated and then shares out a set of

---

2   See, for example, J. Corkindale, *Reforming Land Use Planning*, Institute of Economic Affairs, London, 1998.

3   See, for example, F. Pennance, *Housing, Town Planning and the Land Commission*, Hobart Paper 40, Institute of Economic Affairs, London, 1967; Evans, 1988, op. cit.

4   See, for example, R. Hahn, 'Getting More Environmental Protection for Less Money: A Practitioner's Guide', *Oxford Review of Economic Policy*, vol. 9, no. 4, 1993, pp. 112–23.

pollution quotas for each of the firms operating in the relevant industry. If a firm reduces its emissions *below* its quota level then it can *sell* on the unneeded share of its quota to less efficient firms. Unlike command-and-control methods that mandate particular production techniques and set 'one size fits all' environmental controls, the ability to sell permits provides firms with an on-going incentive to improve their environmental performance rather than simply ensure compliance with fixed government standards. Because the more efficient firms have a positive incentive to continue reducing pollution, there is less need for the state to employ armies of bureaucrats and inspectors to ensure that firms are in compliance with the law. In addition, because firms are free to produce in the manner they see fit, *so long as they do not exceed their given quota*, permits allow a greater degree of flexibility in the production process and allow firms to utilise their own tacit knowledge with regard to the appropriate choice of production techniques, knowledge that might not be available to a centralised regulatory agency.

Tradable-permit schemes have to date mostly been employed with respect to atmospheric pollution control, but in principle there is no reason why they could not be utilised more widely in other areas of environmental policy. Applying the concept of permits in a land-use context would involve the creation of tradable development rights. This might involve a local planning authority setting an agreed level of new development (for example, housebuilding) to be allowed within its jurisdiction and then allocating a set of building quotas between incumbent firms. These firms might then have an incentive to reduce the environmental impact of their developments (by searching out brown-field sites or less attractive green-field sites) so long as they could obtain surplus building quotas, which could then be sold to other firms. As with pollution permits, the advantage of such an approach would be the incentives given to firms to improve their environmental performance and the capacity for them to utilise their own time- and place-specific knowledge with regard to the most appropriate development sites.

While the introduction of tradable development rights may well involve a reduction in some of the regulatory bureaucracy associated with the current planning regime in Britain, this idea is *not*, however, without significant problems of its own. By far the most serious difficulty is the necessity for some form of 'central planning' *in the initial allocation of the permits*. This is likely to be an especially pertinent issue in a land-use context, when compared even with existing tradable-permit schemes for atmospheric pollution control. In the latter case, while some form of arbitrary government planning is involved in deciding the total amount of pollution to be tolerated, there is no need for additional central intervention because the success of firms in improving performance beyond the necessary standards can easily be measured by reductions achieved in the regulated emissions. For land-use planning, by contrast, substantial government discretion would still be required in deciding whether or not firms have actually beaten the relevant 'targets', because these would apply to predominantly aesthetic and hence highly subjective criteria. Deciding, for example, whether firms should be rewarded for having developed a higher proportion of 'brown-field' or 'less attractive green-field' sites would require some preordained criteria to determine what these terms actually mean.

One scheme for the introduction of tradable development rights proposed by Corkindale – the Habitat Transaction Method

– shows very clearly the arbitrariness that would in all likelihood be involved.[5] In Corkindale's scheme, land would be graded on a 1–3 scale, presumably decided at the local authority level, with 3 representing sites of greatest environmental value. As such, this position is scarcely any different from a 'centrally planned' system, even if it is not conducted at the national level. In the final analysis it is the *subjective judgement of the planners concerned* which will determine the relevant environmental grading and *not* the preferences of consumers as expressed through a process of market exchange. The tradable development scheme is thus likely to suffer many of the pitfalls of existing blanket land-use classifications such as the Green Belt, which are lacking in sensitivity to the vast number of local variations in environmental quality that occur *within the designated zones*. One might also add the considerable potential for rent-seeking activities by interest groups in attempting to affect the relevant land-use classifications and the continued potential for bureaucratic expansion that might be associated with the administration of such a regime.

Compensation and the auctioning of development rights

The advocacy of tradable-permit schemes in a land-use context is a relatively new phenomenon in the United Kingdom, but the argument for other so-called 'market-based' policy instruments, and in particular the proposal to 'auction' development rights, has a somewhat longer pedigree. In this instance the aim of reform is to give better incentives to the parties involved in a planning dispute

---

5   Corkindale, op. cit.

to take into account the relevant economic trade-offs that are inevitably involved in any development decision.

One way of introducing such incentives would be to allow the payment of compensation to those adversely affected by a development proposal.[6] Under the present system there is no incentive for those who oppose development in their backyard to take into account the benefits of new development to potential consumers currently outside the area, because there is no prospect of receiving compensation for loss of amenity.

In so far as the British planning system offers *any* compensation it is in the form of so-called Section 106 Agreements. These agreements offer few incentives for those most severely affected by a proposal to consider its wider merits because they *do not* involve *direct financial compensation* to those with the most to lose. Rather, Section 106s require developers to provide 'collective facilities' such as community centres, held to offer benefits to the 'public at large'. In this situation it is not the least bit surprising that people continue to resist development rather than accept 'compensation' in such an inflexible form, which may not accord with their own particular values. Shifting to a model of *direct financial compensation* for those most immediately affected would, therefore, provide greater incentives for the affected parties to come to agreement rather than continue to fight on an 'all or nothing' basis. 'Nimbyist' groupings would then have a material interest in allowing at least some development, and developers themselves would have an incentive to come up with the most environmentally sensitive schemes in order to keep the compensation low.

A further option for reform along these lines that has fre-

---

6   See Evans, 1988, op. cit.

quently been mooted would be to combine the offering of compensation with the auctioning off of development rights. Under this proposal, local authorities would allocate sites for potential development and then sell the rights to the highest bidder. In this situation, those who object to development in a locality would also have the right to bid for the requisite rights. As Veljanovski observes, the attraction of this scheme is that it would ensure that development rights go to those who place the highest value on the land.[7]

Proposals for the auction of development rights do offer a number of attractions and have much to commend them when compared to proposals for tradable-permit schemes. The greatest advantage would be that since people would have the potential to bid for the relevant sites, the resulting land allocations would be more likely to be reflective of consumer preferences. Again, however, it must be noted that these proposals constitute an attempt to reform the planning system *from within*, and may only partially address what continues to be the central flaw of a government system of land-use planning – *the nationalisation of development rights*. 'Auctioning off' development rights involves a form of 'privatisation' on a case-by-case basis, but the bulk of development rights would continue to be vested in the state, and as a result it would be planning authorities themselves that decide *which sites should be put up for auction and the conditions that are to be attached to the sale*. As such, the auctioning process would *not* be subject to a Hayekian process of rivalrous competition between a variety of different sellers. In the absence of the information generated by such competition it would be difficult for planners to know *which sites should*

---

7   C. Veljanovski, Foreword to Evans, 1988, op. cit.

indeed be sold for development purposes and at what particular price. If the nationalisation of development rights is the principal source of failure within a government-administered system, then perhaps the best solution to this problem might be to institute a wholesale privatisation of development rights and thus to shift to a market system of land-use control.

6 LIBERATING THE LAND: THE CASE FOR PRIVATE LAND-USE PLANNING

The previous section called into question the capacity to reform the current land-use planning system without replicating many deficiencies of the existing regime. The analysis presented by both the Hayekian and public-choice perspectives points to major flaws in the arguments that have traditionally been advanced in favour of government land-use regulation. The former suggests that even if planners were immune from self-interest they might lack the informational capacity to 'improve' on the 'imperfections' of land markets. The latter posits that, given the realities of incentive structures in the public sector, land-use planning may be subject to regulatory capture and bureaucratic inefficiency. The question arises, therefore, as to what extent these deficiencies can be addressed by more radical reforms of land-use control, and in particular a shift towards a fully market-driven system.

Coase and private land-use planning

The theoretical case for a private system of land-use planning draws on the work of Coase, which suggests that defining and enforcing an adequate system of property rights so that people can capture the benefits from 'making a market' in externalities may obviate the need for government intervention. If an individual or group owns the right to an environmental characteristic such as a scenic view, then those wishing to develop the area and hence threaten the view may purchase the relevant rights. Likewise, if someone owns the right to develop a piece of land, then those wishing to prevent the development may seek to purchase these rights. According to Coase, the final environmental outcome will be the same *irrespective* of who owns the initial set of property rights.[1]

The Coasian approach has been criticised as irrelevant to many environmental problems because it is held to assume the absence of transaction costs in the definition and enforcement of property rights.[2] It was not, however, the intention of Coase to claim that transaction costs present *no* obstacles to market exchange, but to note the presence of these costs in *any* institutional setting.[3] The argument for relying on private property rights and markets, therefore, stems from the view that, given the informational problems of public planning exposed by Hayek and the 'public choice' problems of government administration, markets, although 'imperfect', may be *more likely* to internalise externalities than the alternative of statutory government planning.

The Coasian perspective suggests that the presence of externality and collective/public goods problems, which are the most frequently cited causes of 'market failure', is the product of the high cost of enforcing property rights. It may be relatively easy for a landowner to exclude non-payers from the benefits of a private

---

1   R. Coase, 'The Problem of Social Cost', *Journal of Law and Economics*, vol. 3, no. 1, 1960, pp. 1–44

2   D. Turner *et al.*, *Environmental Economics: An Elementary Introduction*, Harvester/Wheatsheaf, Brighton, 1994.

3   See, for example, K. Dahlman, 'The Problem of Externality', *Journal of Legal Studies*, vol. 22, no. 1, 1979, pp. 141–62.

park (for instance, by erecting a fence and installing entrance points), but it may be much more difficult for owners to capture the full benefits from the maintenance of clean air, where the externalities are diffuse in character and where the number of potential bargaining parties may be far too great to enable effective monitoring and the enforcement of private contracts. Market failures such as these are a product of high transaction costs, but the market process itself does offer at least some incentives for individuals to devise ways of reducing these costs and to internalise externalities by developing new methods of converting what are currently collective/public goods into private marketable commodities.

Crucially, the existence of transferable property rights in the market provides institutional entrepreneurs with incentives to find ways of increasing the value of different bundles of property rights in order to reap the rewards from their potential sale. As Anderson and Leal note, any case of external benefits/costs may provide fertile ground for an entrepreneur who can devise new ways of defining property rights.[4] The ability of individuals to capture the full benefits and to bear the full costs of their actions is not, therefore, a static phenomenon.

Seen through this lens, rather than have the state act as planner and regulator there may be a strong case for confining the role of government to the enforcement of the evolving contractual bargains struck between private parties and the provision of a legal system that adjudicates disputed property rights in courts. The former role implies that the state concerns itself with discovering

---

4   T. Anderson and D. Leal, *Free Market Environmentalism*, Pacific Research Institute for Public Policy/Westview, San Francisco, 1991.

the wants and desires of the public in order to bring about central planning, an informational impossibility according to the Hayekian perspective. The latter involves government acting merely as a facilitator, strengthening rather than supplanting the market system in its vital knowledge-enhancing role.

Given the deficiencies of government land-use planning, it appears to be an example of what Demsetz termed the 'Nirvana fallacy' to maintain that statutory regulation is essential in order to protect environmental quality, when the alternative to 'imperfect markets' is a system prone to what are potentially more serious institutional failings.[5] What makes the adherence to this fallacy all the more unfortunate is that there may be much greater scope for harnessing the positive aspects of markets than is commonly recognised. There are, in particular, a variety of relatively low-cost transaction methods that can bring environmental values within the realm of the market and might be used to address many of the issues that are currently the preserve of government land-use planning.

Restrictive covenants

In order to understand the basis of a property-rights approach to land-use control, it is important to recognise that the ownership of land does not necessarily refer to *full* ownership of the resource, in the sense of having an *absolute* right to use or dispose of property in any particular way. Rather, it involves ownership of a *bundle* of rights that may be divided up in a variety of different ways. Owners may sell or lease certain rights while maintaining ownership of

---

5   H. Demsetz, 'Information and Efficiency: Another Viewpoint', *Journal of Law and Economics*, vol. 12, no. 1, 1969, pp. 1–22.

others in order to devise a way of increasing the *total worth of the bundle of rights that they possess*.

Within this context, one of the most frequently cited examples of the property-rights approach in a land-use context is the use of private covenants and deed restrictions. In the case of restrictive covenants, developers specify in contracts the activities to be permitted with respect to a particular set of properties for sale, in order to internalise external effects and to capture the returns through higher asset prices. Contractual approaches of this genre may facilitate the creation of markets in amenity values as individuals choose between *competing* developments which offer *different* bundles of contractual restrictions and their associated externalities. Such privatised/contractual forms of planning had a long history of use in Britain before the advent of statutory land-use regulation. Many of the urban developments in Westminster, Hampstead and Oxford, for example, were created through the use of private restrictive covenants.[6] These contractual devices included restrictions on the use of open spaces, noise, chimney smoke and permitted alterations to exterior design. In the United States, meanwhile, covenants have been used in the Rocky Mountains and in parts of the Appalachian chain to preserve the appearance of scenic views.[7]

Like all market solutions, restrictive covenants have the great virtue of delegating authority to the people whose interests are directly involved in the relevant decisions and giving them an economic incentive subjectively to weigh alternatives. When

6   W. West, *Private Capital for New Towns*, Occasional Paper No. 28, Institute of Economic Affairs, London, 1969.

7   T. Anderson and D. Leal, *Enviro-Capitalists*, Rowman and Littlefield, London, 1997.

choosing what sorts of developments they offer, and in particular what contractual restrictions to include, developers interested in increasing the value of their transferable assets have an incentive to consider the opportunity cost of allowing land to be used for some activity *not permitted in the covenant*. Likewise, when considering where to live, consumers have an incentive to weigh the costs and benefits associated with differing levels of amenity protection – higher prices reflecting more restrictive covenants and a greater emphasis on conservation, lower prices reflecting a more lax set of contractual restrictions, etc. In this manner, restrictive covenants may be sensitive to time- and place-specific differences in environmental quality and to individual preferences, with the prices negotiated for different bundles of property rights reflecting the relevant local/contextual variations.

From a property-rights perspective, restrictive covenants also have the virtue of aligning the incentive structures for those involved in land-use disputes in a manner that is more likely to encourage proper consideration of the costs and benefits to society at large. Ultimately, the key to the property-rights approach is that a *price must be paid for the exercise of controls over other people's property*. Those who wish to restrict development in order to preserve amenities have to compete directly in the market for land with others who value the land for alternative uses – and vice versa. Consumers of residential amenity, for example, would have to pay developers directly for the provision of land-use controls via contracts, and would thus be faced with more of the immediate cost of the level of regulation that they are demanding. The primary problem with a government system of land-use planning, by contrast, is precisely that people have *no* incentive to consider the costs associated with the level of regulation demanded (for example, higher prices for consumers) because it is provided as a 'free good' to those with political clout.

Proprietary communities and common property regimes

As a further development of the restrictive-covenant model, Foldvary has advanced the idea of the *proprietary community* as a way for markets to deal with land-use externalities and collective goods problems.[8] Foldvary argues that many collective goods are in practice 'territorial goods' and are, as a result, excludable. The benefits of a scenic view or open space, for example, can often be 'tied in' to the provision of other goods, such as leisure or the purchase of residential environments. So long as the relevant area is privately owned by an individual or group/co-operative, people must reveal their preferences to gain access to such goods through the price system and the free rider/collective good problem can be resolved.[9]

The collective facilities provided by private shopping malls provide a small-scale example of this 'tie-in' concept. Shopping centre merchants provide an array of collective goods through the market, such as malls, security forces, parking lots and a pleasant shopping environment, 'tied in' to the purchase of private merchandise. While competitors could, in theory, enter the market offering comparable private goods at a lower price by not 'tying in' a surcharge for the collective goods,[10] there are many goods whose

---

8   F. Foldvary, *Public Goods and Private Communities*, Edward Elgar, London, 1994.
9   See also J. Buchanan and W. Stubblebine, 'Externality', *Economica*, vol. 29, 1962, pp. 371–84.
10 H. Varian, 'Markets for Public Goods?', *Critical Review*, vol. 7, 1994, pp. 539–57.

value is *contingent* on being provided as part of a package deal.[11]
Thus, shopping centre merchants who do not provide car parking
or a litter collection service might well be able to charge less for
food, but they will also lose the custom of those who value these
services (witness the trend from town-centre to out-of-town shopping in Britain). Likewise, a housing developer who fails to provide
a package of restrictive covenants to protect amenity values will
lose custom to those competitors who do so. As Schmidtz puts it,
'One does not have to be a visionary to realise that market forces
can in theory provide shopping malls, but the point is that there is
no *a priori* reason why similar structural tie-ins could not lead to
the provision of a variety of other public goods as well.'[12]

A useful illustration of the larger-scale provision of collective
goods through contractual ties-ins is provided by the concept of
garden cities, envisaged by the founder of the town planning
movement, Ebenezer Howard. The first settlements proposed by
Howard were to be developed and owned entirely by a private corporation or co-operative, which would plan the design features of
the town, including open-space provision, parkland and landscap-
ing, and then collect the associated revenues in the form of ground
rents. Before the advent of statutory planning and the subsequent
nationalisation of 'new towns', the first garden city in Britain,
Letchworth, was developed on precisely this basis.[13] Similarly, in
the United States, the town of Reston, Virginia, was modelled on
the garden city ideal. The development of the town was financed

---

11 See, for example, Buchanan and Stubblebine, op. cit.; H. Demsetz, 'The Exchange
    and Enforcement of Property Rights', *Journal of Law and Economics*, vol. 7, 1964,
    pp. 127–46; Foldvary, op. cit.; D. Schmidtz, 'Market Failure?', *Critical Review*, vol.
    7, 1994, pp. 525–37.

12 Schmidtz, op. cit., p. 535.

13 See Foldvary, op. cit., for a variety of American case studies.

entirely by the Reston Corporation, a private company, which bought the site and financed the project, including the provision of roads and parks, through the collection of rent. The town has a population of 50,000, housed in 18,000 residential units on a 7,400-acre site. The grounds are landscaped with thickly wooded areas separating the main residential districts, all of which are covered by restrictive covenants.

The property-rights approach set out above is not dissimilar to the proposals for 'common property regimes' outlined by authors such as Ostrom.[14] In the proprietary community model individuals are, in effect, contracting into a set of *collective or shared private property rights* offered for profit by institutional entrepreneurs.[15] In a proprietary community people enter into a voluntary contract to sacrifice complete control over decisions relating to their property to the principles of governance laid down in the proprietary contract. The communities examined by Foldvary, for example, marketed 'constitutional provisions' for the settlement of neighbourhood disputes and laid down a set of rules and procedures (such as voting rules) by which the members of the community could change the terms of collective control. In

14   E. Ostrom, *Governing the Commons: The Evolution of Institutions for Collective Action*, Cambridge University Press, Cambridge, 1990.

15   As is now widely recognised in the property-rights literature, 'common property' regimes are radically different from the 'open access' regimes associated with the 'tragedy of the commons'. The latter refers to a situation where a resource or asset lacks any form of organisational structure with which to manage the resource in question (Ostrom, op. cit.). 'Common property' regimes, however, refer to a position where a resource is managed by some form of co-operative organisation. McKean and Ostrom have described 'common property' regimes as approximating a model of shared private ownership – see M. McKean and E. Ostrom, 'Common Property Regimes in the Forest: Just a Relic from the Past', *Unasylva*, vol. 46, 1995, pp. 3–15.

this sense, the proprietary community provides a mechanism by which externalities and other 'social aspects of living' are internalised by ceding control to a central community 'landlord' who resolves all environmental disputes out of court.

'Integration' through competition

The great advantage of the proprietary-community model is that it may facilitate competition and experimentation between different communities and lifestyles (low-density versus high-density, for example), offering various bundles of collective and individual private property rights and different rules for community management on a range of territorial scales. Which particular mix of individual and common property rights works best cannot be known in advance, but may be discovered over time through a process of entrepreneurial trial and error. Whilst allowing an element of collective control, the property-rights approach provides a clear feedback link to the knowledge and decisions of institutional/property rights entrepreneurs through the account of profit and loss, facilitates consumer choice between an array of property-rights structures and thus enables a discovery process to reveal which particular bundles of land-use restrictions work best in the subjective view of the consumer.

Rather than seeking consciously to 'integrate' the actions of a range of diverse actors into a 'holistic' plan, the property-rights approach may facilitate a wider variety of plans on a range of territorial scales. These 'plans' may then be co-ordinated with one another through the market as the prices paid for differing bundles of property rights/community management structures indicate the relative value placed on environmental assets by society at large. By ensuring that the rewards and penalties of land management are reflected in the relevant community asset prices, the property-rights approach provides the members of such communities with both the information and a direct incentive to weigh up the costs and benefits associated with a range of alternative 'land-use plans'.

Lest it be said that approaches requiring that individuals pay a market price for land-use controls discriminate against those on low incomes, it is worth noting that virtually every study of government land-use planning conducted in both Britain and the United States has concluded that intervention has redistributed wealth from the poor to the middle class.[16] Unlike the relatively easy and cheap comparisons of value between alternatives facilitated by the price system, which can be made by both rich and poor alike, a politicised decision procedure, even when it allows for 'public participation', privileges access to the middle class. These are the groups with the most time to attend endless public inquiries, the most skilled in the use of rhetoric and political persuasion, and who know how best to 'work the system.'[17] In so far as there is a case for actively seeking to 'empower' low-income groups via redistribution, then a far better mechanism would be to do so through the tax system, giving poorer people the resources to spend directly in the market, rather than relying on a complex regulatory regime.

16   See, for example, Hall *et al.*, *The Containment of Urban England*, Allen and Unwin, London, 1973; Simmie, op. cit.
17   See, for example, R. Goodin and J. Le Grand, *Not Only the Poor*, Allen and Unwin, London, 1987.

Tackling the tougher problems: the issue of scale

The analysis set out above indicates the potential for property-rights approaches to tackle a variety of land-use problems, and especially those centred on questions of local amenity. Critics of this model may contend, however, that the approach is limited in applicability to small-scale issues and unable to tackle a range of concerns currently dealt with by government land-use planning which occur over a much wider territorial area. Foremost among these would be the siting of major infrastructure projects such as roads and airports and other public works, which are considered to have 'knock-on' effects or 'network externalities'. According to this view, government planning has an important role to play in co-ordinating the actions of private-sector agents by *lowering transaction costs* in situations where there are a *large number of affected parties*. In order for individuals and firms to make effective investment decisions they may require a degree of 'certainty' as regards the prospective land-use changes brought about by other actors in related markets which may affect the value of their own investments. Without some form of central intervention, in terms of the location of roads, for example, such certainty may not be forthcoming.[18]

As was noted earlier, instances of high transaction costs are indeed a primary cause of 'market failure'. It is, however, crucial to recognise that the competitive market process is a *multi-purpose instrument* which can evolve solutions to deal with the existence of network effects and other externalities that may affect large numbers of actors in a manner that may be more effective than government action. The institution of the business firm is perhaps the

---

18   Report of the Nuffield Foundation, op. cit.

clearest example in point. Firms are 'integrated planning organisations' that develop in situations where there are efficiency gains to be made from replacing the rule of the price mechanism and 'spontaneous order' with a hierarchy of conscious direction that reduces the transaction costs and uncertainties involved in co-ordinating a large number of actors. Rather than have each individual decision conducted on the basis of 'on the spot' contracts, activities within the firm are based to a significant extent on conscious planning mediated through a unified management system and a hierarchy of command.[19]

Within this context, it is important to recognise that the case for the market economy *does not* rest on the assumption of 'atomistic' competition, where there is a 'free for all' in which people can do anything they wish. Rather, the primary argument for the market as advanced by Hayek is that it is a realm of *voluntary planning* characterised by *private property and freedom of contract*. It is within such a realm of private contract that people may voluntarily associate in organisations that restrict their own behaviour in particular ways, in order to engage in acts of planning and social co-operation that can serve the collective good.[20] The proprietors of shopping malls, for example, do not typically allow a 'free for all' on their premises, but define a set of *rules* governing the behaviour of retailers and shoppers alike, in order to benefit all of those who visit the mall. These 'rules' are in turn subject to competition from other proprietors, who may offer different sets of arrangements in order to attract custom.

---

19   Coase, 1937, op. cit. See also R. Coase, 'The Institutional Structure of Production', *American Economic Review*, vol. 82, no. 4, 1992, pp. 713–19.
20   See, for example, D. Klein, 'Planning and the Two Coordinations with Illustration from Urban Transit', *Planning and Markets*, vol. 1, 2000, pp. 1–23.

Seen from this perspective, 'planning organisations' such as firms emerge out of the process of freedom of contract to cope with economic problems such as high transaction costs or externalities/network effects as and when these problems arise. The optimum scale at which the costs of such hierarchies (for example, lack of flexibility due to excessive centralisation) outweigh the benefits (for instance, a unified management system) is itself something that must be discovered and rediscovered, by competition between different types of 'planning regime' *arrived at through private contract*.[21]

In the case of land-use planning, restrictive covenant and proprietary community models could perform functions analogous to those of the business firm and could constitute an effective mechanism for *reducing* transaction costs. By creating a unified management system, the formation of proprietary communities would internalise external effects within a given locality. In addition, the formation of proprietary regimes could act to lower the costs of coping with trans-local externalities where there are a large number of affected parties as the formation of contractual communities reduces the number of contracting parties and facilitates market exchange at the inter-community level. Rather than have large numbers of individuals trying to negotiate with one another over the location of a new trunk road, for example – situations that might well be prone to excessive transaction costs – negotiations could take place between the management boards of such communities, operating so as to increase the value of the relevant proprietary assets. Given conditions of private ownership and freedom of contract, proprietary associations would constitute a *market response* to high transaction costs.

---

21   ibid..

For such an approach to operate effectively would require the radical step of privatising the road network and other local services currently supplied by the state. Indeed, it is a primary implication of this model that local roads should be provided and managed by proprietary communities themselves, and that decisions regarding the location of trans-community routes should emerge through a process of inter-community exchange. Within different proprietary organisations, different approaches may emerge to tackle the land-use externalities associated with road use and other infrastructure. The members of proprietary organisations would thus be required to pay directly for the roads they use by way of a service charge. In turn, the management boards of different communities would be responsible for setting their own rules for road use. Some communities may allow access to road space 'free at the point of delivery', some may introduce periodic traffic bans, whilst others may introduce a system of road pricing. Such decisions would be based upon each association's entrepreneurial judgement of what would constitute the most attractive package from the point of view of potential residents and hence community asset prices.

With regard to trans-community routes, decisions over the location of such infrastructure would be based on a process of *inter-community exchange*. Road developers wishing to build across the territory of a particular community would have to negotiate contracts with the relevant community management organisations, paying a price for the right to build. In situations where trans-boundary effects (such as increased traffic or more noise pollution) arose from the decision of one particular community to allow the development of a new road scheme or other major projects such as new airports, then these could be dealt with by a process of inter-community bargaining. Neighbouring communities could negotiate contracts with one another to internalise the relevant externalities. Alternatively, should such arrangements prove too cumbersome and protracted, then smaller communities might decide to merge in order to form larger management units better able to internalise the relevant externalities in a more 'integrated' manner.

Either way, there would be powerful incentives for private communities to come to mutual agreements and to co-operate with their neighbours on matters of common concern, since a failure to do so would be reflected in declining asset prices. Few people would, after all, wish to purchase property in a proprietary association which insisted that its members drive on a different side of the street from everybody else, just as few people are prepared to purchase mobile phones from providers who do not recognise calls from rival networks. In this manner a market economy of proprietary communities would provide incentives for both competition *and* co-operation. As von Mises argued, it would involve people in an on-going process of 'competing in co-operation and co-operating in competition'.[22]

In the above model, questions of appropriate scale would be dealt with in the same manner as occurs in other markets. If a proprietary community proved too small to gain the advantages associated with increased co-ordination with regard to infrastructure provision such as roads and the internalisation of network effects, then its asset value might be reduced and it might seek to merge with other neighbouring communities. Likewise, if such organisations were to become excessively bureaucratic and cumbersome,

22 Quoted in Klein, op. cit., p. 12.

then smaller, more decentralised communities might start to gain market share and the larger communities might be encouraged to 'downsize' in response to changing market conditions and a fall in their relevant asset prices. In this way, market competition would subject different proprietary structures to a process of trial-and-error evolution, which could adapt in a dynamic way to economic and technological conditions.

From the perspective set out in this paper, there is no one 'optimal' model for reducing transaction costs and network effects; rather there may be a variety of 'competing models'. The proprietary community approach sketched above would, therefore, have considerable advantages over conventional modes of government land-use planning and service provision. Government planning agencies, such as district councils and county councils, are not subject to a process of competitive entry from rival organisational forms and are as a result excluded from a discovery process that can reveal the most appropriate tier of decision-making to internalise network externalities. Similarly, government planning organisations have little incentive to co-operate with one another over questions of trans-boundary externalities or inter-jurisdictional disputes because the financial health of these organisations is *not* sufficiently linked to the achievement of successful co-operation.

While there is no one 'optimal model' of proprietary governance there are, however, strong theoretical reasons for believing that proprietary communities would *tend* to operate on the basis of *smaller* geographical units than do present municipal governments. The bundling together of many services such as land-use planning, fire protection, schools, leisure and recreation, and their delivery by large municipal governments, is largely reflective of the *absence* of competitive forces in the *existing system*. At present, if citizens are dissatisfied with a particular service bundle, then they have no choice other than to leave the relevant town or city. Under the market model, by contrast, it would be much easier for citizens to find alternative service bundles provided on a smaller, more localised scale, as proprietary organisations would be subject to *open competition*. As Klein points out, proprietary communities would probably tend to de-bundle services to discover more specialised market niches, the result being an overall expansion in the number of nearby alternatives and a greater capacity to exercise the option of 'exit'.[23]

A residual role for the state

Notwithstanding the untapped potential for the development of property-rights approaches, there may indeed remain a category of environmental goods where 'market failure' may still be judged to warrant a degree of central intervention – as a 'second-best' approach. Prime candidates would seem to be those ultra-large-scale trans-boundary goods, such as air quality management, where prohibitive transaction costs may continue to be the norm. In these circumstances there may remain a residual role for the state in laying down a set of basic environmental standards and regulations within which the market can be allowed to operate.

What is crucial, however, is that beyond laying down such basic regulatory rules, *no* attempt should be made to co-ordinate land uses according to some holistic plan. Rather, the maximum scope should be allowed for experimentation and innovative property-rights solutions to facilitate co-ordination through the

23   See Klein, op. cit.

forces of markets. The current extent of government intervention in land use far exceeds such minimalist principles, and indeed has actively suppressed the emergence of private property approaches through continued adherence to policy prescriptions that do not allow markets to develop. As Hayek put it so well, to recognise that we may have to resort to direct regulation where the conditions for the proper working of competition cannot be created does not mean that we should suppress competition where it *can* be made to function effectively.[24] The analysis presented above suggests much greater scope for relying on property rights and market processes than is commonly recognised.

24   Hayek, 1944, op. cit., p. 44.

7 CONCLUSION: HOW TO GET THERE FROM HERE

The institutional framework outlined in the previous section would constitute a truly radical departure from the existing planning regime in Britain, involving the wholesale denationalisation of development rights. Given the radical nature of this framework, the question of political feasibility is immediately raised. Because the right to develop land is currently held by the state, the state itself would have to be involved in any attempt to create a new set of property rights in land, and would almost certainly face special-interest resistance from those who gain most from the status quo.

Changing the incentive structure

Probably the biggest winners from the current planning system, and hence those most likely to oppose reform, are those who make up the local amenity/nimby lobby. In order for a property-rights agenda to have any hope of political success, this particular special interest would have to be 'appeased'. The local-amenity interest will vociferously resist proposals to denationalise development rights *so long as these proposals vest the relevant property rights with prospective developers*. Nimbyist interest groups will see the potential for the loss of amenity values that they currently enjoy without the possibility of receiving compensation. This particular incentive structure is, of course, one of the central deficiencies in the current planning regime. It is because of the nationalisation of development rights that people are placed in an 'all or nothing' situation, where they have everything to lose in terms of amenity and property values and nothing to gain by way of financial compensation when decisions regarding land-use changes are made. If a defective incentive structure lies at the heart of the failings of the current land-use planning system, then any programme of reform must be built around a set of principles that can help to change this incentive structure.

In light of the above, one option that might prove attractive in terms of both political feasibility *and* the capacity to restructure individual incentives would be to consider awarding development rights to the communities that are most closely affected by and thus most resistant to development proposals. A case can surely be made that proposals to assign the relevant property rights to local community groups might be positively welcomed. If local communities are given a property right *not* to allow development in a particular locality, through the creation of a proprietary community or restrictive covenants, then immediate opposition to such proposals is likely to subside. Correspondingly, the transfer of property rights from the state to amenity interests may also have a transforming effect on the incentives facing the individuals concerned. If amenity groups hold the rights *not* to allow development *or* to negotiate the terms on which development is to be accepted, then these rights could be *purchased at a price* and under specific contractual restrictions. In this situation the possibility of receiving direct financial compensation for the sale of development rights will give amenity groupings a powerful incentive to weigh the costs and benefits of allowing additional development and maintaining environmental quality in their locality.

The question remains, of course, as to whence such rights are to be derived. At present development rights are divided between private landowners/developers and the state. Landowners hold the right to bring forward land for development, with the state holding the right to accept or refuse such proposals through the granting of planning permission. It is the current owners of land who hold the right to apply for planning permission and hence have the potential to realise substantial capital gains should they be successful in their application. In this situation, those living near by receive *none* of the financial gain should a development be allowed to proceed. If development rights were to be vested with local amenity groupings, therefore, and these groupings were to negotiate payments in exchange for the granting of planning permission, then landowners/developers might be unwilling to accept reform in the absence of compensation for loss of profits.

An immediate issue that arises is that compensation demanded by existing property owners might make this idea prohibitively expensive. It is certainly the case that the prospect of receiving huge financial gains should a large planning application be successful will not be lightly relinquished. With the proliferation of Green Belts and other such regulations, however, the power of the local amenity/nimby lobby is now so great in many parts of the country that, for the majority of landholders, the chances of being successful in such an application are increasingly slim. In this situation many landholders may be open to an institutional alternative, which, while removing the potential for huge capital gains – which exist only on paper under the present system – might increase the likelihood of realising at least some of these gains in practice.

A proposal for proprietary governance

A promising way of moving towards a new system of proprietary governance that might resolve some of the tensions discussed above would be to adopt a variant of a proposal mooted by Moscovitz and O'Toole in the context of Oregon, USA.[1] Moscovitz and O'Toole argue for the local community ownership of conservation easements and restrictive covenants through the creation of *local recreation and amenity companies*. In their proposal, *New Incentives for Rural Communities*, property owners would continue to own their acreage on an individual basis, they would be free to maintain land in its existing use, and they would also have the capacity to bring forward proposals for new development schemes – as at present. *Development rights would, however, be held collectively by all the other property owners encompassed by a recreation and amenity company.*

Under this particular model, the state would divest itself of development rights through the establishment of recreation and amenity companies that would purchase restrictive covenants from participating property owners in a given geographical community, paying for these with the issue of shares in the new company. The company board consisting of all property owners/shareholders in the area would then be responsible for decisions regarding the approval of new development. In turn, *all* profits and losses attributable to such decisions would be *shared out between member property owners, in a manner proportionate to the scale of their holdings*. Individual landowners would no longer hold the right to the full profits from developments on their acreage

1   K. Moscovitz and R. O'Toole, *New Incentives for Rural Communities*, Thoreau Institute, Portland, 2000.

and the state would no longer hold the right to approve or reject development applications. Rather, development rights would become a form of *collective private property right* shared by the members of the recreation and amenity company at the neighbourhood/community level under the auspices of a unified management system.

From the perspective set out in this paper, the great virtue of this proposal is that it provides a way of internalising externalities at the local scale by creating a regime of proprietary ownership. In the Moscovitz and O'Toole model, the value of the proprietary communities' assets would be tied directly to the decisions regarding land management made within its jurisdiction. In contrast to the current British planning system, where the state holds the right to refuse or grant planning permission, under the Moscovitz and O'Toole plan the management board of the proprietary community would itself be responsible for such decisions. Where under the British planning system *all* the profits from a successful planning application go to *individual* landowners proposing new development – but where planning permission may be extremely difficult to acquire for such developments as new housing – under the proprietary model *all shareholders in the community would receive a share of the profits* because development rights would be held by the recreation and amenity company.

As such, the creation of proprietary communities could appeal to both prospective developers and local amenity interests alike. For prospective developers, membership of recreation and amenity companies may bring about a greater likelihood of pursuing successful schemes. While the profits from new development would have to be shared with other members of the proprietary community, the capacity to *realise such profits would be enhanced* because the prospect of local residents receiving a share of the gains would decrease the likelihood of nimbyist opposition on an 'all or nothing' basis. This would apply in the case of both a property owner *within* a recreation and amenity company wishing to develop his or her own individual plot and in the case of an outside developer wishing to purchase and to develop a parcel of land held in common by the proprietary company. Resistance to this proposal and demands for compensation from existing property-owners should thus be minimised, with the offer of shares in the new companies providing a sufficient incentive to join.

For amenity interests, on the other hand, the creation of recreation and amenity companies would invest the power to decide on new development directly in the hands of those most affected. In this situation the property owners concerned could negotiate contractual restrictions to ensure that any development taking place would enhance the asset values of the company in which they hold a share. This would remove the situation where amenity groups have nothing to gain from new development but may be forced to bear the costs.

The above model of proprietary governance would help to frame an incentive structure that would discourage a 'free for all' either on behalf of developers *or* on the part of nimbyist organisations, because property owners/shareholders in recreation and amenity companies would be able to consider decisions in terms of the likely effect on community asset prices. Decisions to prevent any development in the locality would be based on knowledge of the *opportunity cost* of such decisions – that is, the forgone financial gains from allowing new development to proceed. Likewise, decisions to allow inappropriate development and to lower the quality of life within the locality would be taken at the risk of lowering company asset values.

Within this context, recreation and amenity companies would have to exhibit an entrepreneurial sensitivity to market forces. A primary implication of this proposal is that all local services such as road maintenance, the provision of parks and refuse collection, as well as land-use planning, would be the responsibility of the relevant proprietary organisation. Companies would, therefore, have to choose the particular bundle of services they provided and the environmental characteristics they wished to preserve with regard to the attractiveness of such decisions to future residents and hence the likely effect on asset prices. Under these conditions, one would expect to witness a good deal of entrepreneurial experimentation by recreation and amenity boards in an attempt to discover the most desirable mix of environmental characteristics necessary to maintain a competitive edge.

Notwithstanding the theoretical attractions of such an approach there are, of course, a number of difficulties that would have to be overcome if the proposals sketched here were actually to be instigated. Foremost among these would be the need to overcome the so-called 'hold-out' phenomenon, and the difficulty of deciding the appropriate geographical scale at which recreation and amenity companies should be established. In the former instance, an individual property owner might refuse to join a recreation and amenity company if the parcel of land concerned is the last piece of a much larger parcel, in order to obtain a higher proportion of shares issued in the new company. Other members of the community might be willing to pay a higher price for such a plot because if the sale did not take place then all previous purchases would have been wasted. In this particular scenario, the use of 'contingent contracts' would seem to offer the most appropriate solution. These arrangements specify to each individual seller in advance that the contract will not be activated until all other contracting parties have agreed to sign. As a consequence individual owners *do not know* whether they are the first or last prospective seller and the 'hold-out' problem may be resolved.[2]

With regard to the appropriate scale of the new recreation and amenity companies, it is difficult to recommend an 'optimal' size at which the initial companies should be established. As noted previously, one of the most important arguments for a property-rights, market-driven system is precisely that in the absence of a competitive market process it is difficult to know the most effective level at which land-use planning should actually take place. To some extent, therefore, decisions concerning the size of the new companies would have to be made on a somewhat arbitrary basis. That said, some general rules of thumb would seem appropriate, depending on population density and degree of ownership fragmentation in the areas concerned.

It may reasonably be assumed that in rural areas with a relatively low population density the land area covered by the proprietary company might be substantial. This may be necessary where ownership patterns are characterised by the existence of large farms or estates, as is often the case in the more remote upland areas where property holdings tend to be much bigger on economic viability grounds. This particular model may be appropriate in areas such as the National Parks, where owners may also wish to capture recreational returns from individuals *not* residing within the boundaries of the proprietary community itself. One such model might be that of the North Maine Woods Inc. in the

---

2   See, for example, J. Buchanan, 'An Economic Theory of Clubs', *Economica*, vol. 32, 1965, pp. 1–14

United States, a private company formed through an association of twenty landowners. This company manages recreational activities in a 2.8-million-acre park – an area half the size of Wales – with entrance controlled through seventeen checkpoints situated around the perimeter and with fees charged according to the length of stay.[3] In urban and suburban locations, by contrast, proprietary communities should cover much smaller geographical areas, given higher population densities and more fragmented patterns of property ownership. This might involve creating a company at the level of an individual street/group of streets or perhaps at the level of existing parish councils.

Given the inevitable uncertainties involved in deciding the scale at which to create the initial proprietary regimes, it will be important to ensure that an element of flexibility is written into the initial contracts to enable a process of adaptation over time. This would need to include the definition of clear procedures for the members of the proprietary regime to secede from the existing organisation to create a territorially smaller company, or alternatively to merge with a neighbouring community in order to gain the benefits of a unified management system across a larger geographical scale. So long as a set of rules is in place with regard to the process of secession or merger, then it will be possible for a properly functioning competitive market in proprietary planning to emerge between a variety of different organisational forms.

The proposals sketched above present a radical alternative to the continuation of government land-use planning and would clearly require some imaginative thinking if they were to be developed successfully. In many ways, however, such imagination lies at the heart

---

3   Anderson and Leal, 1991, op. cit, p. 69.

of the argument for shifting to a system of private, contractual land-use control. The market economy and the institutions of private property and voluntary contract are remarkably flexible instruments which can respond to an array of social and economic problems if they are allowed to do so. For years, it was suggested that lighthouses could only be supplied by the state, yet as the historical record of successful lighthouse provision by the private sector demonstrates, the imagination of private entrepreneurs is often superior to that of professional economists and planners.[4] The analysis presented in this paper suggests that, given a chance, the entrepreneurial imagination exercised by proprietary communities could deliver equal success in the field of private land-use planning.

Conclusion

After over fifty years of what is the most comprehensive system of government land-use control anywhere in the Western world, it is increasingly evident that the British land-use planning system is ripe for reform. The combined insights of the Hayekian, public-choice and Coasian perspectives applied throughout this paper have been used to highlight some suggestions on which such reform might be based.

---

4   See R. Coase, 'The Lighthouse in Economics', in Coase, *The Firm, the Market and the Law*, Chicago University Press, Chicago, 1989. Coase showed that lighthouses, often considered a collective good by many welfare economists and therefore unlikely to be provided by the private sector, were supplied privately in Britain, before nationalisation. Economists had typically assumed that vessels could benefit from lighthouse facilities irrespective of payment. In fact, lighthouses were provided by harbour companies with fees charged on entrance to the harbour. Those refusing to pay were simply excluded from the port. See also K. Goldin, 'Equal Access vs. Selective Access: A Critique of Public Goods Theory', *Public Choice*, spring 1977.

It has been argued that a combination of decentralisation of planning functions down to the local authority level and the greater use of 'market-based' policy instruments such as the 'auctioning' of development rights may offer considerable advantages over the existing planning regime.

Ultimately, however, this paper has sought to challenge the arguments commonly advanced in favour of a government system of land-use planning and to put the case for a private system of land-use control. Whilst a market system of land-use planning will always be subject to numerous 'imperfections', the analysis presented here suggests that the deficiencies of private markets bear favourable comparison with the failings of the regulatory state. One way or another, there is a need for renewed debate on the future of the land-use planning system. The views advanced in the preceding pages are offered as an invitation to that debate.

ABOUT THE IEA

The Institute is a research and educational charity (No. CC 235 351), limited by guarantee. Its mission is to improve understanding of the fundamental institutions of a free society with particular reference to the role of markets in solving economic and social problems.

The IEA achieves its mission by:

- a high-quality publishing programme
- conferences, seminars, lectures and other events
- outreach to school and college students
- brokering media introductions and appearances

The IEA, which was established in 1955 by the late Sir Antony Fisher, is an educational charity, not a political organisation. It is independent of any political party or group and does not carry on activities intended to affect support for any political party or candidate in any election or referendum, or at any other time. It is financed by sales of publications, conference fees and voluntary donations.

In addition to its main series of publications the IEA also publishes a quarterly journal, *Economic Affairs*, and has two specialist programmes – Environment and Technology, and Education.

The IEA is aided in its work by a distinguished international Academic Advisory Council and an eminent panel of Honorary Fellows. Together with other academics, they review prospective IEA publications, their comments being passed on anonymously to authors. All IEA papers are therefore subject to the same rigorous independent refereeing process as used by leading academic journals.

IEA publications enjoy widespread classroom use and course adoptions in schools and universities. They are also sold throughout the world and often translated/reprinted.

Since 1974 the IEA has helped to create a world-wide network of 100 similar institutions in over 70 countries. They are all independent but share the IEA's mission.

Views expressed in the IEA's publications are those of the authors, not those of the Institute (which has no corporate view), its Managing Trustees, Academic Advisory Council members or senior staff.

Members of the Institute's Academic Advisory Council, Honorary Fellows, Trustees and Staff are listed on the following page.

The Institute gratefully acknowledges financial support for its publications programme and other work from a generous benefaction by the late Alec and Beryl Warren.

117

For information about subscriptions to IEA publications, please contact:

Subscriptions
The Institute of Economic Affairs
2 Lord North Street
London SW1P 3LB

Tel: 020 7799 8900
Fax: 020 7799 2137
Website: www.iea.org.uk/books/subscribe.htm

Other papers recently published by the IEA include:

WHO, What and Why?

Transnational Government, Legitimacy and the World Health Organization
Roger Scruton
Occasional Paper 113; ISBN 0 255 36487 3
£8.00

The World Turned Rightside Up

A New Trading Agenda for the Age of Globalisation
John C. Hulsman
Occasional Paper 114; ISBN 0 255 36495 4
£8.00

The Representation of Business in English Literature

Introduced and edited by Arthur Pollard
Readings 53; ISBN 0 255 36491 1
£12.00

Anti-Liberalism 2000

The Rise of New Millennium Collectivism
David Henderson
Occasional Paper 115; ISBN 0 255 36497 0
£7.50

Capitalism, Morality and Markets

Brian Griffiths, Robert A. Sirico, Norman Barry & Frank Field
Readings 54; ISBN 0 255 36496 2
£7.50

A Conversation with Harris and Seldon

Ralph Harris & Arthur Seldon
Occasional Paper 116; ISBN 0 255 36498 9
£7.50

Malaria and the DDT Story

Richard Tren & Roger Bate
Occasional Paper 117; ISBN 0 255 36499 7
£10.00

A Plea to Economists Who Favour Liberty: Assist the Everyman
Daniel B. Klein
Occasional Paper 118; ISBN 0 255 36501 2
£10.00

Waging the War of Ideas
John Blundell
Occasional Paper 119; ISBN 0 255 36500 4
£10.00

The Changing Fortunes of Economic Liberalism
Yesterday, Today and Tomorrow
David Henderson
Occasional Paper 105 (new edition); ISBN 0 255 36520 9
£12.50

The Global Education Industry
Lessons from Private Education in Developing Countries
James Tooley
Hobart Paper 141 (new edition); ISBN 0 255 36503 9
£12.50

Saving Our Streams

The Role of the Anglers' Conservation Association in
Protecting English and Welsh Rivers
Roger Bate
Research Monograph 53; ISBN 0 255 36494 6
£10.00

Better Off Out?

The Benefits or Costs of EU Membership
Brian Hindley & Martin Howe
Occasional Paper 99 (new edition); ISBN 0 255 36502 0
£10.00

Buckingham at 25

Freeing the Universities from State Control
Edited by James Tooley
Readings 55; ISBN 0 255 36512 8
£15.00

Lectures on Regulatory and Competition Policy

Irwin M. Stelzer
Occasional Paper 120; ISBN 0 255 36511 X
£12.50

Misguided Virtue
False Notions of Corporate Social Responsibility
David Henderson
Hobart Paper 142; ISBN 0 255 36510 1
£12.50

HIV and Aids in Schools
The Political Economy of Pressure Groups and Miseducation
Barrie Craven, Pauline Dixon, Gordon Stewart & James Tooley
Occasional Paper 121; ISBN 0 255 36522 5
£10.00

The Road to Serfdom
The Reader's Digest *condensed version*
Friedrich A. Hayek
Occasional Paper 122; ISBN 0 255 36530 6
£7.50

Bastiat's *The Law*
Introduction by Norman Barry
Occasional Paper 123; ISBN 0 255 36509 8
£7.50

A Globalist Manifesto for Public Policy
Charles Calomiris
Occasional Paper 124; ISBN 0 255 36525 X
£7.50

Euthanasia for Death Duties
Putting Inheritance Tax Out of Its Misery
Barry Bracewell-Milnes
Research Monograph 54; ISBN 0 255 36513 6
£10.00

To order copies of currently available IEA papers, or to enquire about availability, please contact:

Lavis Marketing
73 Lime Walk
Oxford OX3 7AD

Tel: 01865 767575
Fax: 01865 750079
Email: orders@lavismarketing.co.uk